Hanoi
Timeless Top 10 Travel Guides

Hanoi Vietnam Top 10 Tourist Spots, Shopping and Dining, Museums, Activities, Historical Sights, Nightlife, Top Things to do Off the Beaten Path, and Much More!

By Tess Downey

Copyrights and Trademarks

All rights reserved. No part of this book may be reproduced or transformed in any form or by any means, graphic, electronic, or mechanical, including photocopying, recording, taping, or by any information storage retrieval system, without the written permission of the author.

This publication is Copyright ©2020. Nevada. All products, graphics, publications, software and services mentioned and recommended in this publication are protected by trademarks. In such instance, all trademarks & copyright belong to the respective owners. For information consult www.NRBpublishing.com

Disclaimer and Legal Notice

This product is not legal, medical, or accounting advice and should not be interpreted in that manner. You need to do your own due-diligence to determine if the content of this product is right for you. While every attempt has been made to verify the information shared in this publication, neither the author, neither publisher, nor the affiliates assume any responsibility for errors, omissions or contrary interpretation of the subject matter herein. Any perceived slights to any specific person(s) or organization(s) are purely unintentional.

We have no control over the nature, content and availability of the web sites listed in this book. The inclusion of any web site links does not necessarily imply a recommendation or endorse the views expressed within them. We take no responsibility for, and will not be liable for, the websites being temporarily unavailable or being removed from the internet.

The accuracy and completeness of information provided herein and opinions stated herein are not guaranteed or warranted to produce any particular results, and the advice and strategies, contained herein may not be suitable for every individual. Neither the author nor the publisher shall be liable for any loss incurred as a consequence of the use and application, directly or indirectly, of any information presented in this work. This publication is designed to provide information in regard to the subject matter covered. Neither the author nor the publisher assume any responsibility for any errors or omissions, nor do they represent or warrant that the ideas, information, actions, plans, suggestions contained in this book is in all cases accurate. It is the reader's responsibility to find advice before putting anything written in this book into practice. The information in this book is not intended to serve as legal, medical, or accounting advice.

Foreword

With the city's tree – fringed streets, more than a dozen lakes and thousands of French – influenced buildings, the *Paris of the East*, is increasingly becoming a hot spot for tourists.

Located on the banks of the Red River, Hanoi, the capital city of Vietnam and one of the oldest capitals in the world boasts many colonial – era buildings, museums, and ancient old pagodas that will surely captivate any traveller. The people of Hanoi managed to preserve many historical sites that stood the test of time which now complements the hustle and bustle of the city – center.

Hanoi is a place that adventurers can explore on foot, and their culture is something worth experiencing. The city is known for its French – colonial influences particularly on cuisine and architecture – not to mention its vibrant night life, multi – cultural community, lush parks, mountains, villages, handicrafts, and most importantly the famous Ha Long Bay.

The capital of Vietnam has consistently been included in top ten destinations in various surveys including TripAdvisor because apart from its amazing scenery and vibrant culture, it is one of the most affordable tourist destinations that welcome around five million tourists every year.

If this is your first – time visiting the Paris of the East, this travel guide will help you with everything you need to enjoy this French – inspired and multicultural city; from the best accommodations, tourist spots, food, shopping places, museums, historical sites, nightlife, and off – the beaten paths as well as transportation options and travel essentials.

Table of Contents

Table of Contents 5

Welcome to the City of the Soaring Dragon 1

Chapter One: Hanoi Overview 2

    Hanoi in Focus 5

    A Brief History of Hanoi 7

    Language, People and Culture 15

        Etiquette and Customs 16

Chapter Two: Travel Essentials 20

    Traveller's Info 22

    Climate and Weather 25

    Dos and Don'ts's of Visiting Hanoi 26

Chapter Three: Getting In and Around Hanoi 32

    Getting In 33

        From the airport 33

    Getting Around Hanoi 37

Chapter Four: Top 10 Hotels and Accommodations 44

    1.   Splendid Hotel & Spa 46

2. InterContinental Hanoi Landmark 48

3. Serene Boutique Hotel and Spa 50

4. Little Hanoi Deluxe Hotel 52

5. Hanoi La Vision Hotel 54

6. Holiday Emerald Hotel 56

7. La Siesta Hotel 58

8. Hanoi La Siesta Central Hotel and Spa 60

9. Hanoi La Siesta Hotel Trendy 62

10. Hanoi Meracus Hotel 64

Chapter Five: Top 10 Dishes in Hanoi 66

1. Phở Bở 67

2. Bún Chả 69

3. Nom Thit Bo Kho 71

4. Mien Luon 73

5. Ca Phe Trung 74

6. Bun Thang 76

7. Xoi Xeo 77

8. Banh Goi 79

9. Bun Bo Nam Bo 80

10. Ca Phe Cot Dua.. 81

Chapter Six: Top 10 Tourist Spots in Hanoi 84

1. Hoan Kiem Lake.. 85

2. President Ho Chi Minh Mausoleum 87

3. Old Quarter... 89

4. The Temple of Literature 90

5. Dong Xuan Market 92

6. One – Pillar Pagoda 93

7. Vietnam Museum of Ethnology..................................... 95

8. The Imperial Citadel of Thang Long.................... 96

9. Bat Trang Pottery Village... 98

10. Hanoi Opera House 100

Chapter Seven: Top 10 Shopping Places in Hanoi 102

1. Hang Dao Street 103

2. Hang Ma Street.. 105

3. Hang Duong Street 106

4, Van Phuc Silk Village 107

5. Bat Trang Pottery Village 109

6. Parkson Shopping Center 110

7. Vincom Megamall Royal City 111

8. Hang Be Market 113

9. Hang Da Market 114

10. Tet Market 115

Chapter Eight: Top 10 Museums in Hanoi 118

   1.   Air Force Museum 119

   2.   Hoa Lo Prison Museum 121

   3.   Vietnamese Women's Museum 123

   4.   Ho Chi Minh Museum 124

   5.   Vietnam's Fine Arts Museum 126

   6.   Hanoi Museum 127

   7.   Vietnam National Museum of History 129

   8.   B – 52 Victory Museum 131

   9.   Museum of People's Public Security 133

   10.   Vietnam Military History Museum 135

Chapter Nine: Top 10 Nightlife Destinations in Hanoi 138

1. Water Puppet Show 140

2. Hanoi Opera House 142

3. Local Street Food in Hanoi 144

4. Minh's Jazz Club 145

5. The Bank Hanoi 147

6. Hanoi Press Club 148

7. The Vietnam Central Circus 149

8. The Legend Beer 151

9. Dragonfly Bar and Lounge 152

10. Sunset Bar 153

Chapter Ten: Off - Beaten Path in Hanoi 156

1. Propaganda Posters 157

2. 54 Traditions Gallery 159

3. Heritage Walk 161

4. Art Scene 162

5. The Landmark 72 164

6. Vietnamese Museum of Revolution 165

7. Bridegroom Field 167

8. The Bookworm 169

9. Kien Hung Commune 171

10. Vietnam National Museum of Nature 172

Quick Travel Guide 174

3. Hanoi Highlights.. 185

Index 188

PHOTO REFERENCES 190

REFERENCES.. 200

Welcome to the City of the Soaring Dragon

The city of Hanoi is chaotic just like any Southeast Asian metropolis, and sometimes it can be overwhelming for first – timers especially those who have never travelled to Southeast Asian countries before. Hanoi is also the second largest city in the country that has a blend of the West and the East. In addition to French – colonial influences in the past, the city is also heavily influenced with Chinese culture due to centuries of dominance. You will notice that the colonial style buildings were preserved, and weren't

Welcome to the City of the Soaring Dragon

touched by the modern architecture era of the 70's and 80's. Today, the city is undergoing a rapid transformation to make it more modern – looking but still preserve the historical style of the buildings.

The tourist destinations in Hanoi are generally grouped into two quarters; the French Quarter and the Old Quarter. The Old Quarter is located in the Hoan Kiem District that's filled with alleys and small streets where you can easily get the traditional Vietnamese vibe. Many places in this district offer various goods that local vendors specialized in. For instance, you can find various jewelry stores that trade jewelries and silvers in one long alley.

On the other hand, the French Quarters include the southern area of the Hoan Kiem District and the Ba Dinh District which is more of a governmental area since it's where most government offices and headquarters are located such as the Presidential Palace, embassies, administrative buildings, the National Assembly and other ministries. The Old and French Quarters have its own touch of French Colonial style buildings that's perfect for throwback posts in Instagram.

Welcome to the City of the Soaring Dragon

Various historical sites located in Ba Dinh that you can explore include the Ho Chi Minh Mausoleum, One Pillar Pagoda and the Lycee du Protectorat while places such as the Hanoi Opera House, National Museum of Vietnam History, St. Joseph's Cathedral and Sofitel Legend Metropole

Hanoi along with other notable French – Colonial landmarks can be seen in the southern area of the French Quarter in Hoan Kiem District. Many colonial – era buildings in the French Quarter are now used as foreign embassies.

Chaotic as Hanoi can be, it's definitely a city that's filled with character. Once you've walked around the Old and French Quarter, you'll get to experience the eclectic mix of foreign influences and the Vietnamese culture along with the centuries – old history of the city. And I'm pretty sure that if you stick around long enough and be open to the wonderful stories around the corner, you'll surely enjoy your stay here.

Welcome to the City of the Soaring Dragon

Chapter One: Hanoi Overview

Hanoi being the second largest metropolis in Vietnam (next to Ho Chi Minh City) has a population of around 10 million people as of this writing. The city can be found in the northern region of Vietnam and it is near the Red River delta around 56 miles away from the coastal area.

When it comes to topography, the city of Hanoi has three kinds of land terrain; delta area, midland region, and mountain zone. These terrains are slightly lower from the north going to the south, and from the west going to the

Chapter One: Hanoi Overview

east; the average height is around five to twenty meters above sea level. The mountain and hill zones are situated in the western and northern areas of the city. The highest peak in Hanoi is at 1,281 meters specifically at Ba Vi which can be found in the western area of the metropolis.

The Old Quarter as mentioned earlier is the hub of tourists from around the world. In addition to visiting landmarks and historical places, you can immerse in the Vietnamese culture once you've strolled along the streets and alleys of the Old Quarter. There are lots of hotels, markets, dining places, malls, bars, club, cafes and tons of street food vendors that you can sink your teeth into to taste what Hanoi has to offer. Unlike in other cities like Tokyo or LA, the Old Quarter in Hanoi is not that spread out which means everything is walking distance. Many tourists just spend around 2 days (tops) in the city before moving to the French Quarter.

You may also find that the city of Hanoi doesn't have breathtaking skylines unlike in other Southeast Asian cities. Buildings in the metropolis are usually just five - stories tall, but you can still see towering skyscrapers if you go to Ho Chi Minh which is just a few miles away from Hanoi.

Chapter One: Hanoi Overview

In addition to this, you may also notice that there are LOTS of motorbikes in the city (around 80% of Vietnamese use motorbikes as the main form of transportation), and crossing the street may feel like playing with death because there are no designated pedestrian lanes. This is something that most tourists find overwhelming especially if they came from the west where there are stoplights and street lanes everywhere. Don't worry though because the drivers will just go around you, and pretty soon you'll get the hang of it. Just walk in the same pace when crossing roads or better yet go along with other people who are also crossing the street.

Chapter One: Hanoi Overview

Hanoi in Focus

During the ancient times, invading forces around the city agree on one thing: Hanoi is a great capital. According to historians, the city has held that title for many centuries. It has undergone many invasions and name changes. In 1408, Chinese conquerors sieged the Dai La which is the imperial city of Vietnam and change its name to Tong Binh. In 1428, Le Loi fought against foreign invaders and eventually changed the name of the city yet again to Le Thai To. Fast forward to 1831 during the time of the Nguyen Dynasty, the city was given the name Ha Noi. However, the power was transferred to Hue and it became Vietnam's capital for a

Chapter One: Hanoi Overview

while until the country was invaded by French. The French officially made Hanoi the capital of Indochina. Around 1954, the city was ceded to Ho Chi Minh after a decade of fighting the French army, and Hanoi eventually became the capital of North Vietnam. It was only in 1975, when the city of Hanoi was officially declared as the capital for the whole country.

The city of Hanoi retained much of its French – influenced colonial vibe despite the various invasions and battles that befall upon it. Such conflicts made it largely untouched by modern architecture which is why most building is just five – stories high. If you want to see more French – inspired places, you can go to Hoi An where there are lots of well – preserved colonial and pre – colonial architecture that will sort of take you back in time. Many foreign expats reside in Tay Ho which is also located in the metropolis. Tay Ho is home to many English teachers, foreign restaurants, and the signature Pho dish of Vietnam.

As you walk along the bustling streets of Hanoi, you may encounter that locals try to strike up a conversation with you, that's because it's a norm for them to talk to strangers and may ask you general questions. This overt

Chapter One: Hanoi Overview

friendliness can be very helpful especially if you get lost but still practice caution and be alert.

A Brief History of Hanoi

Before Hanoi became known as the "Paris of the East" and before it became one of Southeast Asia's beautifully preserved colonial – era city, it had gone through different significant events throughout history. Let's take a look back at it:

Van Lang Dynasty

- **300 B.C.E:** A region in Van Lang formed an area known as Giao Chi which is now the present – day Hanoi is situated.
- **258 B.C.E:** Au Viet which is under the Shu Pan emigrant conquered Van Lang.

Au Lac Dynasty

- **257 B.C.E.:** Shu Pan established Co Loa and made it the capital of Au Lac's unified kingdom. It is the present – day Dong Anh district.

Qin Dynasty

- **214 B.C.E:** The first emperor started his campaign to fight that people of the south which is also known as Baiyue.
- **208 B.C.E.:** General Zhao Tuo defeats Shu Pan and took over Co Loa. General Zhao Tuo incorporated Co Loa to the Nanhai Commandery.

Nanyue Dynasty

- **204 B.C.E:** General Tuo declares Nanyue as an independent kingdom.
- **196 B.C.E.:** Lu Jia secures a nominal submission of the kingdom to Han
- **179 B.C.E.:** The lands of the Nanyue kingdom in the Red River Valley have already been organized under the command of Giao Chi.

Han Empire

- **111 B.C.E.:** The commander of Giao Chi submits to Han and remained in his post to begin the first northern domination of Vietnam.
- **208 C.E.:** Long Bien erected in its eponymous district

Chapter One: Hanoi Overview

- **226 C.E.:** Roman embassy arrives

Song Dynasty

- **454 – 464 C.E.:** Songping was established in the Hoai Duc and Tu Liem Districts by the Liu Song which is situated on the south bank of the Red River.

Van Xuan Dynasty

- **544 C.E.:** Long Bien became the capital of Ly Bi under the Van Xuan dynasty.

Tang Dynasty

- **621 C.E.:** Songping and Long Bian to prefectural status
- **722 C.E.:** Songping was defeated by Mai Thuc Loan
- **866 C.E.:** The local jiedushi called Gao Pian expands its fortress at Jincheng and was renamed as Big Enclosing Walled City.

Dai Viet Dynasty

- **1010:** Thang Long erected the Imperial Citadel and dedicated the capital to the Ly Dynasty.

Chapter One: Hanoi Overview

- **1049:** The One Pillar Pagoda was erected
- **1070:** The Temple of Literature was built
- **1076:** The Imperial Academy was established

Medieval Period

- **1225:** The city becomes capital of the Tran Dynasty
- **15th Century:** The Quan Su Temple and Temple of the Jade Mountain was built.
- **1408:** The city was renamed to Dongguan during the Ming Dynasty in China.
- **1573:** The Foggy Lake was renamed as the West Lake.
- **1802:** Hue became Vietnam's capital.
- **1831:** The city was renamed Ha Noi ("Between Rivers") by Minh Mang, a Nguyen Emperor.

French Occupation (19th to 20th Century)

- **1873:** Francis Garnier takes citadel
- **1874:** The concession of France was granted via treaty.
- **1882:** French officially occupied Vietnam.
- **1883:** the Battle of Cau Giay and Battle of Phu Hoai took place near the city.

Chapter One: Hanoi Overview

- **1886:** The Turtle Tower and Kinh Thien Palace were built
- **1887:** Banque de l'Indochine opens in Vietnam
- **1888:** St. Joseph's Cathedral built
- **1890:** Operation of Steamboat starts on the Red River
- **1894:** Lanessan Hospital was built for the French Army
- **1898:** the Hoa Lo Prison and the Geological Museum was built
- **1900 – 1902:** The École française d'Extrême-Orient established its headquarters in Hanoi. Hanoi became the capital of French Indochina. The railway station opens and the Indo China Exposition World Fair was held.
- **1911:** Hanoi Opera House was built.
- **1929 - 30:** Vietnamese Communist Party was organized in Ham Long Street and the headquarters was established in Tho Nhuom.

Chapter One: Hanoi Overview

Japanese Occupation

- **1941:** On December 7, Japan officially occupied Vietnam
- **1942:** Ba Dinh District (formerly Hoan Long District) becomes part of the capital.

French Re - Occupation

- **1945:** Japanese occupation ends. On September, Ho Chi Minh reads the Proclamation of Independence of the Democratic Republic of Vietnam in Ba Dinh Square. Tran Van Lai becomes the mayor; Voice of Vietnam starts airing and the National Library of Vietnam established and Vietnam National University.
- **1946:** National Assembly had a meeting in the Great Theatre. On December, the Battle of Hanoi started.
- **1947:** Around February, the Battle of Hanoi comes to a conclusion with French remaining in power.
- **1951:** Hanoi National University of Education was established.

Chapter One: Hanoi Overview

Democratic Republic of Vietnam

- **1954:** Hanoi became the capital of North Vietnam. Hanoi Radio starts airing.
- **1956:** The Vietnam School of Music, Hanoi University of Science and Technology and the University of Agriculture and Forestry were established.
- **1958:** The National Museum of Vietnamese History was established. Thanh Nien Road was constructed.
- **1959:** Vietnam Military History Museum was inaugurated, Hanoi University of Foreign Studies and the Vietnam Museum of Revolution was established.
- **1965:** Residents started evacuating Hanoi on threat of airstrikes by the U.S. forces.
- **1966 - 67:** Aerial bombing outside the city by the U.S. forces along with air battles between North Vietnamese army and the U.S. army.
- **1970:** Vietnam Television starts broadcasting
- **1972:** Aerial bombing by the U.S. forces.
- **1976:** Hanoi becomes capital of Socialist Republic of Vietnam.
- **1978:** Noi Bai International Airport officially opened.

Chapter One: Hanoi Overview

- **1980:** Hanoi Institute of Theater and Cinema was established
- **1984:** Vietnam National Symphony Orchestra was revived
- **1989:** The population in the city reaches 1 million.
- **1993:** Vietnam War Memorial was erected and Hanoi University of Science was established.
- **1997:** Organisation internationale de la Francophonie summit took place
- **1998:** Hang Day Stadium opens
- **2003:** Hanoi hosted meeting of Asian Network of Major Cities
- **2005:** Hanoi Securities Trading Center was launched. On November, the Asia – Pacific Economic Cooperation was held.
- **2009:** The 2009 Asian Indoor Games was held.
- **2010:** This year marks the Millennial Anniversary of Hanoi
- **2018:** There were protests against proposed special economic zone legislation.

Chapter One: Hanoi Overview

Language, People and Culture

Vietnamese is the official language of the whole country. It is a tonal language that is quite similar to Khmer which is Cambodia's official language. With each syllable, there are 6 different tones that are being used which may also change the definition, something that foreigners have a hard time understanding.

Other languages are also spoken in Hanoi and in the entire country including Chinese, Cham, and Khmer as well as other local dialects spoken by tribes living in the mountain zone. In written form, the Vietnamese language uses the Roman alphabet and uses accent marks to show

Chapter One: Hanoi Overview

tones. The writing system is called Quoc Ngu. The Quoc Ngu was created and used around the 17th century to translate the Catholic scriptures. This writing system also replaced the Chu Nom and had been the unofficial writing system for many centuries.

Etiquette and Customs

The Vietnamese society has many public etiquette that any foreigner or tourists need to keep in mind. The following are the most common customs and etiquette in Hanoi and in Vietnam:

- As much as possible, try to avoid PDAs or public display of affection with the opposite sex especially in religious places.
- Do not touch someone's head for no reason
- You must pass the items with both hands as a sign of respect
- Don't use your finger when pointing, use your hand instead.
- Don't stand with your hands on your hips and cross your arms as it can be considered rude.

- Don't pass anything over someone's head and don't touch a person on the shoulder
- Shorts must only be worn at the beach or in private places.

Dining Etiquette

If you are invited over to a Vietnamese home, you should bring incense, flowers, or fruits. The gifts you bring should be wrapped up nicely. Don't give yellow flowers, handkerchiefs or anything inappropriate. When it comes to table manners, you should wait for the host to show you where you should sit. For the Vietnamese, the oldest person sits first. When passing dishes, you should use both of your hands. Chopsticks are the most common utensil used; it should be placed on the table after every few mouthfuls or whenever one is speaking or drinking. It's a norm among locals to hold bowls close to their faces when eating or sipping the soup.

Try to eat all the food on your plate and avoid ordering excessive food you can't handle. Once you're done, you should place your chopsticks on top of the rice bowl. Make sure to cover your mouth using a toothpick.

Business Etiquette

When it comes to setting appointments, it's required to make it several weeks or days in advance. One of the best means of setting up an appointment is through a local representative that can also be a proxy and/ or interpreter. Take note that the Vietnamese are punctual so make sure to not be late. You should dress conservatively especially when attending a business meeting. Handshakes are usually used upon meeting for both men and women. Sometimes they use a two – handed shake wherein the left hand is on top of the right wrist. If you are a man, you must wait for a woman to extend her hand for a handshake; otherwise you can just bow your head. Business cards are usually exchanged during business meetings, and it should be offered with both hands. When someone presented you a card, make sure to properly receive it and don't just leave it anywhere else.

Chapter One: Hanoi Overview

When it comes to hierarchy, the most senior is the one who should enter the room first though it will vary within business meetings. It's also important to note that silence is quite common in meeting especially when someone disagrees so as not to lose face. For Vietnamese people, building relationships are very important when it comes to business partnerships so always try to maintain a good relationship with your potential partners. The spoken word to them is also very important; you should not make promises you can't keep. When it comes to negotiations, keep in mind that it can be slow because Vietnamese people take their time when taking decisions, and it needs to go through lots of consultation as well as government approvals (if any) so be patient.

Chapter Two: Travel Essentials

Most locals in Hanoi don't know how to speak English, and even if some of them do, they only know a few words except some workers in tourist hubs like hotels, restaurants, and offices. College students can speak English but they aren't that fluent either compared to other Asian countries. This is why you may want to study some basic Vietnamese as it may come in handy when you're travelling in the city.

Chapter Two: Travel Essentials

You may also find locals in the metropolis quite lazy and they're not in a rush – you'll see lots of them just chilling outside, or just drinking tea and spitting sunflower seeds in street curbs. You'll also encounter tiny tables and chairs in local food places as if the customers are in pre – school. There are lots of backpackers in the city including Americans, Europeans and Australians. The city is increasingly becoming popular with other foreign nationals because of its very friendly culture.

This chapter will include all the essentials you need as a traveller including money exchange, credit card and electricity information, the best time to go, the communication services available including the public holidays you need to observe. We also included a list of don'ts when visiting this bustling city so that you will stay safe and equip you with all the things you need to make this trip an awesome experience.

Chapter Two: Travel Essentials

Traveller's Info

Check out in this section the important things you need to keep in mind before you travel in Hanoi.

Currency

The currency in the city and in the entire country is Vietnamese Dong. As of this writing, the exchange rate is $1USD = 23,195 Vietnamese Dong (VND). If you withdraw money from the ATM, you'd feel like a millionaire because a dollar is exchanged into lots of dongs but of course the value is still the same. Everything in the metropolis follows a cash only basis though some high – end places may accept credit cards/ debit cards. We highly recommend that you have twice as much money as you need so as not to turn your trip into a hassle.

The best part of travelling around the city is that everything is cheap and it is perhaps the cheapest capital in Asia. Your two dollars can already give you a bowl of the Vietnamese signature dish called Pho, a taxi ride around the city, and a shirt – with change to spare! The best part is that you can also bargain items like souvenirs especially if you're buying from a street vendor.

Chapter Two: Travel Essentials

Electricity and Voltage

When it comes to voltage, the standard electricity voltage in the country is 220 Volts at 50Hz. You can use your devices as long as the label says that it is "50 – 60Hz" or "100 – 240 volts." It is compatible provided that you have the right plugs.

If you are coming from Japan and Central or North America, the device you are using may only have 110 volts. To make your device work, you need to buy a transformer to convert the voltage and make it compatible. You can purchase adapters or converters in various convenient stores as well as bookstores. It may cost you around $4 or more.

Public Holidays

Every day is the best time to travel to the Paris of the East, but for your convenience; do take note of the following dates and events so you can plan ahead and avoid any hassle. The public holidays listed below means that institutions such as banks, government offices, museums and some businesses are closed or they're only open for a few hours.

Chapter Two: Travel Essentials

- **New Year** (1 January)
- **Tet Holiday and Valentine's Day** (February 14)
- **Vietnamese New Year's Eve** (February 15)
- **Vietnamese New Year** (February 16)
- **Tet Holiday** (February 17 – 20)
- **March Equinox** (March 20)
- **Hung Kings Festival** (April 25)
- **Liberation Day** (April 30)
- **Labor Day** (May 1)
- **June Solstice** (June 21)
- **Independence Day** (September 2)
- **September Equinox** (September 23)
- **Vietnamese Women's Day** (October 20)
- **Halloween** (October 31)
- **December Solstice** (December 22)
- **Christmas Day** (December 25).

Communication Services

- **Mobile Phones/Telephones**

The telephone code in Hanoi is 4. However, do keep in mind that the number 3 should be added in front of the local numbers. Check out the example below:

Chapter Two: Travel Essentials

- - Dial 3 (+local number) from within the city, or 04 (+local number) for inter – provincial calls. Dial +84 4 (+local number) from overseas calls.

- **Wi-Fi/ Internet Services**

You can find lots of internet cafes around the city. Most internet cafes are used by teenagers and you'll see them just playing online games and battle games. The rates will vary but it can start for as low as 3,000 dong per hour. You'll also find slightly high – end internet cafes in the Old Quarter where most tourists are, and they have computers that are capable of video calls and international phone calls. You can also connect to the Wi – Fi of restaurants/ dining places as long as you order something. There are many Wi – Fi hubs in Hoan Kiem Lake as well.

Climate and Weather

Hanoi has a warm and humid subtropical climate with lots of rain showers throughout the year. The city has 4 seasons and it also experiences similar to other areas in northern Vietnam. Summer in the city is quite hot and humid with abundant precipitation; it starts from May 'til August. The fall season which is characterized by decrease in rainfall and temperature starts from September 'til October. Winter which is cool and dry starts in November and lasts until January. It's also usually foggy and cloudy during winter time that extends through February and March.

You shouldn't schedule your trip during the rainy season which is from May to September. The average temperature in the city is 23°C with a humidity of around 79%. The highest recorded temperature is around 42°C back in 1926, while the lowest is 2.7 °C back in 1955.

Dos and Don'ts's of Visiting Hanoi

Below is a list of do's and don'ts that can guide you to some of the social norms and taboos during your trip. Keep in mind these pointers, and you'll surely have a socially and culturally enriching experience!

Chapter Two: Travel Essentials

DO'S

- Do store your cash, tickets, credit/ debit cards as well as other valuables in a secure place. Most hotels have in – room safety boxes. You may also opt to ask the reception area to keep your valuable things using their deposit facility for a period of time.

- We highly suggest that you get the hotel business card from the reception desk before you go out so that it'll be easier for you to return if you're going to ride a taxi or other mode of transportation.

- Always bring along with you a toilet paper especially if you're going to take a trip because you'll never know when you're going to need it!

- Always dress appropriately especially if you're going to visit culturally sensitive areas or places of worship such as pagodas and temples. Vietnamese are conservative when it comes to dress codes. Try not to wear revealing clothing and wear proper attire depending on the occasion.

- Make sure to drink lots of bottle water so as not to get dehydrated especially if you visit the city during the summer. Try to drink at least 2 liters of water per day and if you constantly drink coffee, tea or alcohol make sure to also increase your water intake.

- If you get invited into a Vietnamese household, make sure to remove your shoes at the front door.
- Always ask for permission if you're going to use the restroom and properly excuse yourself. It's also better to ask if you can take photos on the places you will visit.

DON'TS

- Always be aware of pickpockets and bag snatchers. Don't wear too much flashy things such as jewelries or flaunt your gadgets around so as not to attract potential robbers. Also, it's very impolite to flaunt such bling – blings in public. On the other hand, you don't need to be paranoid but just like in any other places you go to exercise vigilance and caution.

- Don't wear shorts, skirts, low – neck lines, and other revealing clothing especially when going to sacred places as it can be considered offensive and rude.

- Don't give away candies, water bottles, or other plastic materials to locals especially if you find yourself trekking through minority villages because they may not know how to properly dispose it. Most ethnic people have no access to various basic needs so if you want to donate, it's better to coordinate with appropriate authorities or leaders in the community.

- Never sleep with the feet of your soles pointing to the family altar if for instance you will be sleeping in someone else's house.

- Don't lose your temper in public to avoid trouble or lose face. Try to maintain a happy and cool demeanor. Be patient and understanding.

- Don't take photos of anything that has to do with the military (unless you're allowed) as it can be a breach of national security.

- Don't take videos of the ethnic groups when going to minority villages as it can be intrusive to the locals.

Chapter Two: Travel Essentials

Chapter Three: Getting In and Around Hanoi

Chapter Three: Getting In and Around Hanoi

As mentioned in previous chapters, tourists will only need 1 to 2 days to see the entire city of Hanoi. Hanoi can be travelled around by foot or if you would like to have some sort of "wild" adventure, you may want to try renting a motorbike since this is their main mode of transportation around the city. This chapter will provide with you with information on how you can get in the city from the airport, and also give you transportation options on how you can tour around the metropolis and experience first - hand its hustle and bustle.

Chapter Three: Getting In and Around Hanoi

Getting In

From the airport

Taxis

There are lots of taxis waiting outside the 'Arrival' area at the airport in Hanoi. You just need to turn to your right if you're coming from the domestic terminal, or turn left if you're landing from international terminal. All the taxis in Hanoi are run by meter, and they are provided by different cab companies. We highly suggest that you have the address written down of your hotel or the place you'll go to so that you can just present it to the driver because the chances of you communicating with each other effectively is very slim since most of them don't speak or understand English well. You can also print out a map or use apps to guide you in the streets of Hanoi as you go along.

The estimated cost of going to the Old Quarter from the airport is 300,000 to 350,000 dong (around 28 km distance on the meter). If you're going to the French Quarter from the airport, it may cost a little more but still less than 400,000

Chapter Three: Getting In and Around Hanoi

dong. Some drivers will ask more than 400,000 dong if they see more than 2 foreigners, but just ignore them. Make sure to check the meter as you begin the ride. It will only take 30 to 40 minutes from the airport to Hanoi but may take a bit longer depending on the traffic.

We highly recommend that if you already booked a stay in your hotel, you can ask them to dispatch you a driver, and just put the fare on your room bill – this way you are much safer and you won't get ripped off.

Express Buses

You can opt to take express buses from the airport as well. It's going to be a 45 to 60 minute travel time going to the city – center since buses will still have to stop at their designated stations. Bus 86 usually takes the expressway all the way up to the first stop which is the Tay Ho area followed by the Long Bien station, Opera House, Melia Hotel and Rail Station. The bus arrives every 25 minutes, and runs from 6:20 AM to 11:00 PM. As of this writing, it may cost you 30,000 dong to get from the airport to the city – center. From the international terminal, you can find the

Chapter Three: Getting In and Around Hanoi

express bus at pillar 2, second road near the arrivals area. You just have to turn left after exiting the international terminal.

If you're coming from the city – center going to the airport, express buses starts at 5:05 AM until 10:40 PM. You should go to the booth located at the south end of the main railway station.

Public Buses

If you choose to take public buses, it'll take you around 90 minutes or more before arriving to Hanoi. You can take Bus 07 as it crosses the Thang Long Bridge and heads up to the western area of Hanoi which is about an hour away from the central area of the city. Bus 17 crosses the Chuong Duong Bridge and comes near the Old Quarter and the Hoan Kiem Lake area where most tourists stay. As of this writing, the price of public buses is 9,000 dong.

To catch the public buses, you need to head over to the first floor of the terminal, go outside and find the bus parking lot since this is the end stop of the bus routes. You just need to follow the incoming buses if in case you have

Chapter Three: Getting In and Around Hanoi

trouble finding where they are parked. Baggage is not allowed though you can give the conductor a small bribe as payment for your baggage.

Train

Trains use the main station (located in Ga Hang Co) for daily services in and out of the city not just Hanoi but also Saigon, Lao Cai, Nha Trang, Hue and others.

Tickets for all destinations in Vietnam are sold at the main station and the ticket booth is divided into two; the north and south counters which serves their respective cities. There is a queuing system at Hanoi Station but in reality, no one is following such system. Locals disregard it and it's actually quite chaotic. You will see passengers pushing their way to the counters to get train tickets.

We highly recommend that you purchase tickets as soon as you can because some sleeper tickets can be sold out easily. If you can't buy a ticket, you can go to a travel agent and see if they still have any, or try your luck at the station just a few minutes before boarding time because some agents hold and sell it for a slightly higher price. According

Chapter Three: Getting In and Around Hanoi

to many tourists and travel experts, travel agencies in Hanoi have a bad reputation when it comes to business practices. They often overcharge customers up to 300% which is why it's best to just buy the ticket straight from the train station or check out the real price so that you'll know if you're getting ripped off.

Getting Around Hanoi

By Foot

Travelling the city of Hanoi through walking is perhaps the best way to see its beauty. You can traverse small alleys and streets in the Hoan Kiem lakeside as well as the Old Quarter where there are lots of landmark and activities to do. From the Old Quarter, it's around 1.5 to 2 km stroll towards the West Lake and the Ho Chi Minh complex. Make sure to follow the local rules on traffic safety although you'll soon find out that nobody is following traffic rules so be very careful especially whenever you're crossing the streets.

Chapter Three: Getting In and Around Hanoi

The Churong Durong or the southern bridge across the Red River is for vehicles only and doesn't have any sidewalk. On the other hand, the northern bridge or the Long Bien is where motorbikes and pedestrians can travel. You'll get to see impressive structures including small plantations as you stroll along the Red River.

By Cyclo - Taxi

Cyclo – taxis are not cars but more of a 4 to 7 – seater motorbikes. Within Hanoi, there are 3 companies that are reliable; the Taxi Group (which is Hanoi Taxi and CP Taxi) are color white, the Mai Linh which are color green, and the Taxi NoiBai but they specialize in airport transfers and not in getting around the city. We highly suggest that you ask your hotel to dispatch you a reliable cyclo – taxi to prevent any rip – offs because cyclo – taxis in Hanoi have quite a bad reputation as well when it comes to pricing. Some drivers automatically demand 200,000 dong for just 100 meter. You can try to haggle and get tangled up with their language but if that's how you're going to get a lower fare then consider all of that as part of the Hanoi experience. Just be careful of

Chapter Three: Getting In and Around Hanoi

common scams which are defective meters, robbery and roundabout routes. Some will pretend to help you and translate but will later ask for a fee.

If you like a flat fee, it's best to use the app GrabTaxi which functions just like an Uber. You can just input your destination, agree on the price and book it. GrabTaxi drivers only accept cash as payment. You can also choose to opt a meter which can cost you around 20,000 dong for the first 2 kilometers. You don't have to tip them but it's up to you.

By Motorbike Taxis

You can choose to ride a motorbike taxi particularly if you're staying the Old Quarter since they're almost at every corner. However, don't try to find them because if they see that you do, they will try to increase the price, so show only faint interest. You should haggle and firmly agree on a fix price to avoid being ripped. It's best to write down the fare and get an okay from the driver – this will serve as your receipt as well. Once you get one, the driver will give you a helmet.

Chapter Three: Getting In and Around Hanoi

We highly recommend that you use the app GrabTaxi and choose the motorbike option as a form of vehicle as it's usually cheaper and you can pay a flat rate without the need for haggling.

If you're going to travel from Hoan Kiem Lake to Ho Chi Minh's tomb, the travel time is around 10 minutes and the cost should not be more than 20,000 dong. Once you get to your destination, make sure to not let them wait for you because they will charge you with a lot of dongs!

Motorbike Rental

If you prefer driving on your own while soaking in the chaotic motorbike town of Hanoi, you can rent one for $6 to 7 per day. Your hotel may also help you with the arrangement. This is great if you know how to ride one, or if you will like to make lots of trips around the city. A word of caution though, we cannot emphasize how chaotic and undisciplined the drivers are in Hanoi. All of them don't follow the rules, and there are also no pedestrian lanes. Some drivers will always cut you off, and people will constantly just cross the street so make sure to be extra

Chapter Three: Getting In and Around Hanoi

careful because the city is not the place to practice your motorcycle skills. When you're parking, make sure to lock the front wheel and park in places with other bikes. Some shops have bike attendants that'll give you a parking ticket and the fee may cost between 2,000 and 5,000 dong.

The ticket may have a number so you or the attendant can easily locate the bike, or in other shops it contains your license plate number. Sometimes, the bike attendants may ask you to not lock the front wheel so they can easily move the bikes as customers come and go.

By Bus

There are also buses that can tour you around the city which are cheap and usually scam – free. However, the problem is that signs and the conductor can be hard to comprehend and you may get lost if you don't know exactly where you're going. Hanoi buses are fast and comfortable but still be careful of pickpockets and other petty crimes.

Make sure to pick up the bus line map which can be found at the Trang Tien Street or by the book street near the Opera House. Identify the lines and the routes before going

Chapter Three: Getting In and Around Hanoi

to the bus stop. Wait for the bus to arrive and pay the fare. As of this writing, it may cost you 7,000 dong. You can also inform the conductor on where you're going or need to get off so that he can inform the driver. You can also use Google Maps or other GPS apps to keep track of the road. Bus lines may not arrive on time due to traffic jams so be patient when waiting.

Chapter Three: Getting In and Around Hanoi

Chapter Four: Top 10 Hotels and Accommodations

The best hotels in the city are located in the commercial district of Hoan Kiem. The landmarks and historical sites are practically walking distance including the Opera House, Ngoc Son Temple, Hoan Kiem Lake and the National Museum of Vietnamese History among others. As previously mentioned, the city – center is where the Old Quarter is where most tourist spots can be found. You can stroll around the area especially in the northern region because this is where you can find various local shops, art

Chapter Four: Top 10 Hotels and Accommodations

galleries, temples, colonial – style buildings, night market and the likes.

On the southern area is where you can find the French Quarter where affluent tourists usually stay. This is where you can find five – star hotels, luxury malls, high – end bars and restaurants as well as foreign embassies not to mention the awe – inspiring colonial and pre – colonial architecture. Lodging in the city of Hanoi caters to just about any traveller; there are many charming guesthouses for those on a budget and luxury hotels for the affluent tourists. All of which have nice guestrooms, onsite amenities, amazing customer service and best of all, an easy access to everything Hanoi.

In this chapter, we have listed the top 10 best hotels and accommodation in the city that's perfect for backpackers and for those who may want to splurge a bit during their stay.

Chapter Four: Top 10 Hotels and Accommodations

1. Splendid Hotel & Spa

This hotel is only a four to 10 minute walk to the famous Thang Long Water Puppet Theatre and the Hoan Kiem Lake. There's a round - trip airport shuttle provided by the hotel that's available for 24 hours though there is an automatic surcharge. Main amenities include guestrooms, complimentary breakfast and newspaper, restaurant, business center, 24 – hour front desk, daily housekeeping and laundry service, toiletries, computer station, airport shuttle, front desk safe, air condition and free Wi – Fi among others.

Location: Hà Nội, Hoàn Kiếm, Ngõ Hàng Hành District Vietnam,

Chapter Four: Top 10 Hotels and Accommodations

The Splendid Hotel & Spa is walking distance to the following landmarks and places:

- Hoan Kiem
- 2 minute walk to Dong Kinh Nghia Thuc Square
- 3 minute walk to Hang Gai Street
- 4 minute walk to the night market (open on weekends)
- 4 minute walk to the Thang Long Water Puppet Theatre
- 5 minute walk to Ta Hien Street
- 7 minute walk to Ngoc Son Temple
- 7 minute walk to Thang Long Ca Tru Theatre
- 8 minute walk to Hang Da Market
- 8 minute walk to Vietnamese National Tuong Theatre
- 8 minute walk to Bach Ma Temple

Chapter Four: Top 10 Hotels and Accommodations

2. *InterContinental Hanoi Landmark*

This hotel is targeted for tourists who want to splurge on their accommodation or for those who have meetings with potential business partners. They also have facilities to accommodate company meetings as well as seminars or small conferences. There's also a round – trip airport shuttle that's available for 24 hours and free valet parking. In addition to that they feature other amenities like business center, spa, outdoor pool and gym.

Main amenities include more than 300 smoke – free guestrooms, fine – dining restaurants, health club, garden, outdoor and children's pool and full – service spa, airport

Chapter Four: Top 10 Hotels and Accommodations

shuttle, daily housekeeping, 24 – hour business center and front desk, free valet parking and Wi – Fi. They also offer free cribs for families with infant and you can also book adjoining rooms for the whole family or for colleagues.

Location: Keangnam Hanoi Landmark Tower, Plot E6, Cau Giay Urban Area, Từ Liêm, Hà Nội 100000, Vietnam

The InterContinental Hanoi Landmark 72 is walking distance to the following landmarks and places:

- 1 minute walk to AON Hanoi Landmark Tower
- 13 minute walk to Vietnam National Convention Center
- 22 minute walk to My Dinh National Stadium
- 28 minute walk to Vietnam Museum of Ethnology
- 33 minute walk to Lotte Center Hanoi

Chapter Four: Top 10 Hotels and Accommodations

3. *Serene Boutique Hotel and Spa*

The Serene Boutique Hotel and Spa is located in the heart of the Old Quarter specifically in the Bat Su area where most tourists are. This affordable hotel is very easily accessible to the hustle and bustle of the city – center and tourist spots. It's also just an hour away to the Noi Bai International Airport. The Serene Boutique hotel provides lodgers a comfortable place to stay in after a day spent exploring the wonderful city of Hanoi. There are various rooms that will suit the budget of any traveller and they also offer extensive range of facilities that guests will surely enjoy.

Chapter Four: Top 10 Hotels and Accommodations

Main amenities include more than 45 guestrooms, mini bars and lounges, childcare, airport shuttle services, housekeeping and laundry services, concierge services, banking services, front desk safe, toiletries, complimentary breakfast and free Wi – Fi.

Location: Old Quarter, 16-18 Bát Sứ, Hàng Bồ, Hoàn Kiếm, Hà Nội, Vietnam

The Serene Boutique Hotel and Spa is walking distance to the following landmarks and places:

- Hoan Kiem
- 3 minute walk to Hang Ma Street
- 5 minute walk to Vietnamese National Tuong Theatre
- 6 minute walk to Bach Ma Temple
- 6 minute walk to Night Market
- 7 minute walk to Ta Hien Street
- 7 minute walk to Hang Da Market
- 7 minute walk to Dong Xuan Market
- 8 minute walk to Hang Dau Water Tower
- 8 minute walk to Hanoi Old City Gate
- 8 minute walk to Hang Gai Street

Chapter Four: Top 10 Hotels and Accommodations

4. Little Hanoi Deluxe Hotel

Another great hotel that's quite affordable for backpackers is the Little Hanoi Deluxe Hotel. It's quite small with only 15 guestrooms available so if you want to stay here, it's best to book in advance especially if you're going to Hanoi during peak season or holidays. Amenities include guestrooms, 24 – hour room service and front desk, airport shuttle and concierge services, daily housekeeping and laundry services, luggage storage, tour assistance, toiletries, minibar and air condition.

Chapter Four: Top 10 Hotels and Accommodations

Location: 1 Yên Thái, Hàng Gai, Hoàn Kiếm, Hà Nội, Vietnam

The Little Hanoi Deluxe Hotel is walking distance to the following landmarks and places:

- Hoan Kiem
- 1 minute walk to Vietnamese National Tuong Theatre
- 4 minute walk to Hang Da Market
- 4 minute walk to Hang Gai Street
- 7 minute walk to Dong Kinh Nghia Thuc Square
- 7 minute walk to Night Market
- 8 minute walk to Ta Hien Street
- 9 minute walk to Hang Ma Street
- 9 minute walk to Thang Long Water Puppet Theatre
- 10 minute walk to Bach Ma Temple
- 10 minute walk to Thang Long Ca Tru Theatre

Chapter Four: Top 10 Hotels and Accommodations

5. *Hanoi La Vision Hotel*

Hanoi La Vision Hotel is another slightly affordable accommodation that's perfect for those travelling with families or in groups. It's only 15 minutes away from the famous Ho Chi Minh Mausoleum and the Temple of Literature. Amenities include round – trip airport shuttle, housekeeping and dry cleaning services, luggage storage and front – desk safe, lockers, complimentary breakfast, ticket assistance, car rentals and other usual hotel utilities.

Location: 19 Bát Đàn, Hàng Gai, Hoàn Kiếm, Hà Nội 100000, Vietnam

Chapter Four: Top 10 Hotels and Accommodations

The Hanoi La Vision Hotel is walking distance to the following landmarks and places:

- Hoan Kiem
- 3 minute walk to Vietnamese National Tuong Theatre
- 5 minute walk to Hang Ma Street
- 6 minute walk to Hang Da Market
- 6 minute walk to Night Market
- 7 minute walk to Ta Hien Street
- 7 minute walk to Hang Gai Street
- 8 minute walk to Bach Ma Temple
- 8 minute walk to Dong Kinh Nghia Thuc Square
- 9 minute walk to Thang Long Ca Tru Theatre
- 9 minute walk to Hang Dau Water Tower

Chapter Four: Top 10 Hotels and Accommodations

6. *Holiday Emerald Hotel*

The Holiday Emerald Hotel is near the Hanoi La Vision Hotel with pretty much the same amenities and affordable rates. It's also just a few minutes away from the Hoan Kiem Lake where you can stroll at night to see the beautiful scenery with all the lights and cold breeze. In addition to a round – trip airport shuttle, they also have a train station pick – up service. It has 21 smoke – free guestrooms with terrace, daily housekeeping and dry cleaning services, 24 – hour front desk and front desk safe to attend to your things upon arrival, high – end restaurants, tour assistance, cable TV, complimentary breakfast and free Wi – Fi to keep you connected.

Chapter Four: Top 10 Hotels and Accommodations

Location: 24 Hàng Mành, Hàng Gai, Hoàn Kiếm, Hà Nội 100000, Vietnam

The Holiday Emerald Hotel is walking distance to the following landmarks and places:

- Hoan Kiem
- 2 minute walk to Vietnamese National Tuong Theatre
- 3 minute walk to Hang Gai Street
- 4 minute walk to Hang Da Market
- 6 minute walk to Dong Kinh Nghia Thuc Square
- 7 minute walk to Night Market
- 8 minute walk to Thang Long Water Puppet Theatre
- 8 minute walk to Ta Hien Street
- 8 minute walk to Hang Ma Street
- 10 minute walk to Bach Ma Temple
- 10 minute walk to Thang Long Ca Tru Theatre

Chapter Four: Top 10 Hotels and Accommodations

7. La Siesta Hotel

La Siesta is a peaceful hotel where every tourist will feel at home. It's also the newest project of the Elegance Hospitality Group so you can expect modern interior design and luxurious ambience inside the hotel apart from their personal service. It is located at the old Ma May Street which is just walking distance from major tourist spots and the Hoan Kiem Lake. It embodies a modern style with a touch of colonial Hanoi and the guestrooms range from duplex to spacious bedrooms that's perfect for families, backpackers, and group of friends. In addition to basic amenities and

Chapter Four: Top 10 Hotels and Accommodations

facilities they also include mini bar and lounge, full – service spa, restaurants, childcare, fitness center, common area where you can have snacks or coffee, and adjoining rooms.

Location: 94 Phố Mã Mây, Hàng Bạc, Hoàn Kiếm, Hà Nội, Vietnam

The La Siesta Hotel is walking distance to the following landmarks and places:

- Hoan Kiem
- 1 minute walk to Thang Long Ca Tru Theatre
- 5 minute walk to Night Market
- 5 minute walk to Hanoi Old City Gate
- 5 minute walk to Thang Long Water Puppet Theatre
- 5 minute walk to Bach Ma Temple
- 6 minute walk to Dong Kinh Nghia Thuc Square
- 7 minute walk to Ngoc Son Temple
- 7 minute walk to Ceramic Road
- 7 minute walk to Hang Gai Street

Chapter Four: Top 10 Hotels and Accommodations

8. *Hanoi La Siesta Central Hotel and Spa*

The Hanoi La Siesta Central Hotel and Spa is an alternative option if the La Siesta Hotel is already full – booked especially during peak season or holidays. It's also a few minutes away to major attractions like the Thang Long Water Pupper Theatre and it also has a great relaxing ambience that tired tourists can come home to after a day spent in the city. Services include 24 – hour front desk, bar and lounge, concierge services, multi – lingual staff, complimentary breakfast, housekeeping services, spa services, free cribs for infants and other amenities.

Chapter Four: Top 10 Hotels and Accommodations

Location: 1 Cầu Gỗ, Hàng Bạc, Hoàn Kiếm, Hà Nội 100000, Vietnam

The Hanoi La Siesta Central Hotel and Spa is walking distance to the following landmarks and places:

- Hoan Kiem
- 1 minute walk to Thang Long Water Puppet Theatre
- 3 minute walk to Dong Kinh Nghia Thuc Square
- 3 minute walk to Ngoc Son Temple
- 4 minute walk to Thang Long Ca Tru Theatre
- 4 minute walk to Ta Hien Street
- 5 minute walk to Night Market
- 5 minute walk to Hang Gai Street
- 5 minute walk to Ceramic Road
- 6 minute walk to Hanoi Municipal Party Committee
- 8 minute walk to Bach Ma Temple

Chapter Four: Top 10 Hotels and Accommodations

9. *Hanoi La Siesta Hotel Trendy*

The Hanoi La Siesta Hotel Trendy is another branch of the Elegance Hospitality Group that offers basic amenities and services at an affordable price. It's also walking distance to major tourist attraction in Hanoi and features around 40 guestrooms. Amenities include restaurants, bars, spa services, childcare, airport shuttle, housekeeping and laundry services, concierge services, multilingual staff, toiletries and other facilities that every guests will surely appreciate.

Chapter Four: Top 10 Hotels and Accommodations

Location: 12 Nguyễn Quang Bích, Cửa Đông, Hoàn Kiếm, Hà Nội 100000, Vietnam

The Hanoi La Siesta Hotel Trendy is walking distance to the following landmarks and places:

- Hoan Kiem
- 2 minute walk to Vietnamese National Tuong Theatre
- 4 minute walk to Hang Da Market
- 7 minute walk to Hang Ma Street
- 7 minute walk to Hang Gai Street
- 10 minute walk to Night Market
- 10 minute walk to Dong Kinh Nghia Thuc Square
- 10 minute walk to Ta Hien Street
- 11 minute walk to Hanoi War Museum
- 11 minute walk to Lenin Park
- 12 minute walk to Flag Tower of Hanoi

Chapter Four: Top 10 Hotels and Accommodations

10. *Hanoi Meracus Hotel*

Last but not the least is the Hanoi Meracus Hotel which is also located near the Hoan Kiem Lake. It has great ambience though there are only 13 guestrooms available. It's quite a cozy place with complete amenities and services such as complimentary breakfast, dry cleaning and laundry, round - trip airport shuttle, tour and ticket assistance, luggage storage, and free Wi – Fi.

Location: 32 Hàng Trống, Hoàn Kiếm, Hà Nội, Vietnam

Chapter Four: Top 10 Hotels and Accommodations

The Hanoi Meracus Hotel 2 is walking distance to the following landmarks and places:

- Hoan Kiem
- 5 minute walk to Hang Gai Street
- 6 minute walk to Dong Kinh Nghia Thuc Square
- 7 minute walk to Trang Tien Plaza
- 8 minute walk to Thang Long Water Puppet Theatre
- 8 minute walk to Hang Da Market
- 8 minute walk to Weekend Night Market
- 8 minute walk to Vietnamese National Tuong Theatre
- 9 minute walk to Ta Hien Street
- 9 minute walk to Vietnam Women's Museum
- 10 minute walk to Ngoc Son Temple

Chapter Five: Top 10 Dishes in Hanoi

Vietnamese cuisine has captured the hearts and culinary tastes of famous chefs around the world including Gordon Ramsay and the late Anthony Bourdain including former U.S. President Barack Obama. That being said, what better city to have a taste of this Indochina flavor than Vietnam's capital! Hanoi's bustling streets and alleys may confuse the inexperienced traveller when it comes to searching the right food spot in the city which is why in this chapter, we will guide you in finding the best sources of dishes Hanoi has to offer that both tourists and locals highly recommend.

Chapter Five: Top 10 Dishes in Hanoi

Below is the top 10 favorite dining spots and world – class dishes that will surely keep you coming back for more. Dig in!

1. Phở Bở

You've never been to Vietnam if you haven't tried a bowl of the country's signature dish, Phở Bò. It consists of rice noodles served with beef slices that both locals and tourists love. The broth came from meat, beef bones, lime and fresh herbs sprinkled with lemon zest. In addition to these ingredients, it also comes with bean sprouts for that

Chapter Five: Top 10 Dishes in Hanoi

extra crunch as well as chili that will surely tingle in your tongue with delight.

One of the best dining places that offers a scrumptious bowl of Phở Bò is called Phở 10. This no – frill dining place is easily recognizable because of its brusque signboard that says 'Pho' – a perfect place for a quick yet delicious meal. The restaurant offers the basic Phở Bò dish with half – done beef slice (*bo tai*), or you can choose a *bo chin* which contains a well – done beef brisket for just 70,000 dong or around $4. This restaurant is the go – to place to satisfy that Phở Bò cravings.

Location: 10 Lý Quốc Sư, Hàng Trống, Hoàn Kiếm, Hà Nội, Vietnam

Chapter Five: Top 10 Dishes in Hanoi

2. *Bún Chả*

Bún chả or vermicelli with pork appears quite simple until you taste it. This flavorful dish is compose of grilled fatty pork and vermicelli topped with sweet and sour sauce that brings together its complex flavor. When in Hanoi, we suggest that you eat this dish as the Vietnamese do.

Try the northern way of consuming it through mixing the vermicelli with the broth then sip it just like how you would eat a bowl of noodles. Or you can have this meal the southern way by rolling the beef with a piece of lettuce and dip it in some sauce to enhance its meaty flavor.

Chapter Five: Top 10 Dishes in Hanoi

Earning a nickname of "bun cha Obama" is Bún Chả Hương Liên. It is perhaps one of the best places in the country if you want to try this delectable meal. It rightfully earned its nickname as it recently went viral online since this is where former U.S. President Barack Obama and the late celebrity chef Anthony Bourdain dined together. If it's good enough for a president, it's probably good enough for any tourists like you! After finishing off your bowl of amazing *bun cha*, don't forget to take a picture of the now glass – encased table where the president and the late famous chef dined in!

Location: 24 Lê Văn Hưu, Phan Chu Trinh, Hai Bà Trưng, Hà Nội, Vietnam

Chapter Five: Top 10 Dishes in Hanoi

3. *Nom Thit Bo Kho*

The Nộm Thịt Bò Khô or dried beef salad is a mixture of green papaya, dried beef, roasted peanuts and fresh herbs dressed with fish sauce and lime. For those who are on a diet or you just want to simply have a light and quick meal then this low calorie – dish is definitely for you.

Long Vi Dung is one of the best dining places in the city that offers Nộm Thịt Bò Khô. The restaurant is just walking distance to Hoan Kiem Lake and the Thang Long Water Puppet Theater, so if you want to take a break from

Chapter Five: Top 10 Dishes in Hanoi

strolling along Hanoi's bustling Old Quarter you can head on over to Long Vi Dung for a quick meal.

Locals and tourists love going to here because they also offer other versions of the dried beef salad; you can also order chewy beef with peanuts top off with minty zest and coriander. The restaurant also serve other dishes such as nem chua (fermented pork rolls) and nom chim (pigeon salad) if you want to try something different.

Location: 23, Hồ Hoàn Kiếm, Hàng Bạc, Hoàn Kiếm, Hà Nội, Vietnam

Chapter Five: Top 10 Dishes in Hanoi

4. *Mien Luon*

Mien Luon may not be for everyone but if you're not afraid to taste something new and actually delicious, why not try eating eel noodles for a change?

Chomping down slithering creatures like an eel may not arouse any appetite but a bowl of mien luon might be just enough to change your mind. This dish also comes with glass noodles that are made out of cassava flour along with a soup from eel bones and ginger. This meal is not just exotically delicious but also surprisingly nourishing!

There's no other place that offers *Mien Luon* than *Mien Luon* restaurant itself! This tiny restaurant is found at the

Chan Cam Street where lots of locals come to eat in true Vietnamese fashion. They also offer other dishes but the deep – fried eel cooked to perfection along with the flavorful eel broth is their specialty and a favorite among Hanoians.

Location: 1 Chân Cầm, Hàng Trống, Hoàn Kiếm, Hà Nội, Vietnam

5. Ca Phe Trung

Cà Phê Trứng or Egg Coffee is introduced by the French around the 19th century when they occupied the country. It has since become one of the major products for

Chapter Five: Top 10 Dishes in Hanoi

export in the country. The city of Hanoi boasts their robust coffee culture and offers variety of Vietnamese coffee from drip to weasel and *luwak* coffee. Egg coffee is composed of a strong black coffee that's topped with condensed milk and foamy cream made out of egg yolk. One sip of this delightful mix will make you come back for more!

There are various cafes in the city that offers Cà Phê Trứng but Café Pho Co is the go – to place if you want to try this bizarre mixture of coffee and egg. It's one of the best cafes in Hanoi and they also offer other delightful, must – try flavors. The quirky café is filled with Chinese furniture, assorted potted plants, and bird cages that exhibit an eclectic ambience. Millennials love taking Instagram - worthy photos because of the cafes' perfect setting. Another coffee shop that offers the best Cà Phê Trứng is Giang Café.

Location: 11 Hàng Gai, Hàng Trống, Hoàn Kiếm, Hà Nội, Vietnam

6. Bun Thang

A bun thang or ladder noodle is a traditionally made dish that's usually being served during the *Tet* or Vietnamese New Year on February 5. Locals aren't sure of the origins of the dish's name but many chefs suggest that it points to the satisfaction that one gets after eating the meal – that when you sip the sweet broth of the bun thang, it's similar to an ascending stepladder towards pure bliss because of the soup's flavorful mix. The meal consists of over 20 ingredients that include shiitake mushrooms, dried shrimps, and chicken meat complemented with cucumber, egg, ham slices and some onions.

Chapter Five: Top 10 Dishes in Hanoi

The best place to get this hearty dish is a restaurant called Bún Thang Bún Bung. The restaurant is near Hoan Kiem Lake that will surely make you comfortable and relaxed amidst the swirling traffic of the city.

Location: 32 Cầu Gỗ, Hàng Bạc, Hoàn Kiếm, Hà Nội, Vietnam

7. Xoi Xeo

Xôi Xéo or Vietnamese sticky rice has a shade of turmeric – yellow that's often served with fried shallots and mung beans. This dish is a favorite among the working – class because it will surely fill up your tummy just by eating a single bowl – not to mention its affordable price.

Chapter Five: Top 10 Dishes in Hanoi

Xôi Xéo is a densely packed rice that has layers of hand – peeled mung bean which you can get in a restaurant called Xôi Yến. This dining spot has great interior design that will make your dining experience very memorable. You have an option to choose a tasty side dish like a salted pork to complement the sticky rice. The staff may not speak or understand English but their menu does come with translations for tourists. Enjoy the shallots and bean that comes in a steaming bowl of Xôi Xéo with pickled cucumber on top.

Location: 35B Nguyễn Hữu Huân, Hàng Bạc, Hoàn Kiếm, Hà Nội, Vietnam

Chapter Five: Top 10 Dishes in Hanoi

8. *Banh Goi*

Bánh Gối or pillow cake is a golden brown and deep-fried dish that's quite greasy but definitely flavorful. It's quite similar to a fried dumpling because it contains minced pork that is wrapped up in Indochinese empanadas. It's a snack that also comes with fresh herbs, mushrooms and some black fungus.

The best place to get a Bánh Gối is a restaurant called Quan Goc Da located in the charming Old Quarter. Order this light snack and see how hot oil fries the dis to your satisfaction. Let this scrumptious and cheap snack fuel you as you stroll along the streets of the busy capital.

Location: 52 Lý Quốc Sư, Hàng Trống, Hoàn Kiếm, Hà Nội, Vietnam

Chapter Five: Top 10 Dishes in Hanoi

9. *Bun Bo Nam Bo*

Bún Bò Nam Bộ is a southern – style beef noodle dish that's also included as one of the many beef – based cuisines of Vietnam. What makes this dish unique from other signature Vietnamese bowls like *thit bo kho* and pho is that the beef slices are marinated and soaked in sauce that consists of fish sauce, delectable seasonings, pepper and sugar. It's also served with cucumber, bean sprouts and vermicelli topped with cilantro and grounded peanuts for that extra crunch. The Bún Bò Nam Bộ has long been a staple dish in Hanoi.

The go – to place for this dish is patterned after its name which is called Bún Bò Nam Bộ restaurant. The interior design of the dining spot is simple, with only lines of

Chapter Five: Top 10 Dishes in Hanoi

benches and metal tables for their customers, but their bowls of Bún Bò Nam Bộ definitely says a lot. Expect to see endless orders from the counter both from tourists and locals alike because it's that savory and appetizing. Finish the meal off with a cold beer and don't forget to mix it before eating so that the beef slices can absorb the restaurant's secret sauce.

Location: 67 Hàng Điếu, Cửa Đông, Hoàn Kiếm, Old Quarter, Hoan Kiem Hà Nội, Vietnam

10. Ca Phe Cot Dua

Last but definitely not the least is Cà Phê Cốt Dừa or coconut coffee. It's a milky and tasty drink that's made out of coconut milk, condensed milk and strong Vietnamese

Chapter Five: Top 10 Dishes in Hanoi

coffee that will surely kick – off your morning! This drink is a great start for any tourists preparing to tour around the busy streets of Hanoi or give you a buzz after a long day of strolling in the city.

The best place to get this tasty drink is Cộng Cà Phê. It has many branches all over Hanoi so you'll surely never run out of this sweet coffee fix. Their staff sports a red and greed Viet Cong uniforms and each drink is served in a cool military chic; you'll also get to enjoy the charismatic atmosphere while you're drinking you Cộng Cà Phê which is often served with shaved ice.

The café also feature balconies where you can have the best view of Old Quarter's busy alleys and the nearby Hoan Kiem Lake, a perfect spot to relax or take an Insta-worthy photo with family and friends. You may also want to try their tantalizing *ca phe cot dua* drink as you observe the sea of Hanoian crowd below.

Chapter Five: Top 10 Dishes in Hanoi

Chapter Six: Top 10 Tourist Spots in Hanoi

Hanoi's centuries of civilization always attracts foreigners around the world at the sight of its vibrant ambience and ancient features. A tour around the city will definitely leave a lasting impression on tourists and make them come back for more. The bustling capital of Hanoi attracts not just international visitors but also locals every year because of its historical sites, authentic Vietnamese cuisine, interesting places and friendly culture. The city also houses the most number of relics in the country that can surely make any history buff interested.

Chapter Six: Top 10 Tourist Spots in Hanoi

It is a great place to go to especially when it comes to spiritual and cultural tourism development, or if you simply want to immerse yourself into its fascinating blend of ancient and modern uniqueness. In this chapter, we'll take a look at the top 10 most popular and highly recommended tourist destinations in Hanoi.

1. Hoan Kiem Lake

Don't you dare miss going to Hoan Kiem Lake which is located in the heart of the city! The formerly called West Lake is a symbol of Hanoi's capital and it should be one of the first stops of any tourists like you. If you want to

Chapter Six: Top 10 Tourist Spots in Hanoi

momentarily get away from the hustle and bustle of Hanoi, the quiet, peaceful and refreshing air of Hoan Kiem Lake is a great place in experiencing that sought – after tranquil moment. In addition to the beautiful scenery, you can also visit other landmarks surrounding the lake like the Ngoc Son Temple, Turtle Tower, the Huc Bridge and the Pen Tower. The Ngoc Son Temple was erected for the commemoration of Tran Hung Dao, a 13th – century military leader who was renowned for his courage during the battle against the forces of Yuan Dynasty.

Both the surrounding landmarks and the side of the lake offer lots of shaded spots thanks to its many lush trees. The Hoan Kiem Lake will surely refresh you and give you a chance to relax after a long day of strolling in Hanoi's busy alleys and streets.

If you want to visit the landmarks around the Hoan Kiem Lake, there's a booth around the area where you can buy tickets that costs around 30,000 VND which comes with a tour guide. Make sure to follow the tour guide and comply with the regulations of the temple especially when it comes to attires. The area is open every day from 8:00 AM to 5:00 PM.

2. *President Ho Chi Minh Mausoleum*

Ba Dinh Square is another one of the most visited places in Hanoi specifically the mausoleum of President Ho Chi Minh. It's a historic place because it is where President Ho read Vietnam's Declaration of Independence on September of 1945 which established the Democratic Republic of Vietnam. The mausoleum, consists of three layers and measures around 14 ha, was inaugurated in August of 1975, and it's is also where the president's body is resting.

Chapter Six: Top 10 Tourist Spots in Hanoi

The shape of the mausoleum is patterned after a lotus flower with bamboo figurines on both sides and orchards as it symbolizes Vietnam's countryside. In front of the tomb is a flagpole that's about 30 meters high along with 18 trees that line both sides. You can see the carving of President Ho Chi Minh on top of his tomb filled with rubies. The tomb was the product of Vietnamese and Russian artists.

You can also view the historic Ba Dinh Square from the mausoleum but don't take photos because electronic gadgets may not be permitted. Visitors must follow the regulations inside the tomb particularly the dress code. It is open five days a week except on Mondays and Fridays.

Chapter Six: Top 10 Tourist Spots in Hanoi

3. Old Quarter

One of the reasons why the city has attracted lots of foreign and local visitors is because of the famous Old Quarter which consists of more than 36 century – old, narrow - styled streets and various alleys that's filled with ancient housing architecture (antique brick houses with tiled roofs and pipes). The pace of life in the city is very rapid but the Old Quarter appears otherwise. It is situated in the city – center and very well – known for its lines of local street foods, colonial – inspired architecture, history and friendly neighborhood.

Chapter Six: Top 10 Tourist Spots in Hanoi

The Old Quarter was formed around the 11th century bringing visitors back to the past and giving them a glimpse of what life is like in those days. It's a chance for you to discover the traditional custom and culture of the city and also the whole country. It's best to go here every Saturday so that you can witness folk arts activities like Tuong, Cheo and Quan ho as well as performances from the Vietnam Musicians Association.

4. *The Temple of Literature*

The Temple of Literature or Van Mieu – Quoc Tu Giam is known as "the first university in Vietnam." It's just

Chapter Six: Top 10 Tourist Spots in Hanoi

about a few minutes away from the Hoan Kiem Lake. It is a renowned historical site in Hanoi as it contains the quintessence of feudal historical periods of the country.

The Temple of Literature preserved the traditional value of the Vietnamese for many centuries and also a combination of the ancient and modern era which is why it has become the pride of Hanoians and Vietnam.

It was built in 1070 during the reign of Emperor Ly Thanh Tong and was one of the temples in the country that's dedicated to famous scholars and sages like Confucius before becoming a place where students can train and foster their intellectual talent. You can also check out more than 80 tombstones of around 1,000 Ph.D students who went there and took part of 82 exams from 1442 to 1779. The tombstone can be found above the backs of the tortoise carving where their names and place of birth are engraved. The entrance cost 10,000 VND or $0.50 and it is open every day except on Mondays from 8:30 AM to 11:30 AM and 1:30 PM to 4:30 PM.

Chapter Six: Top 10 Tourist Spots in Hanoi

5. Dong Xuan Market

Another tourist attraction that was constructed in 1889 is the Dong Xuan Market. It is one of the largest and oldest market place in the city that's filled with various stalls selling an array of Vietnamese goodies including clothing, fresh foods, home appliances, souvenirs and the likes. Dong Xuan Market mainly served tourists unlike other markets in the country; it also opens at night until early morning. One of the most striking characteristics of this market place is the historical events that took place like the battle that happened between the French and Vietnamese forces. Tourists also have an opportunity to communicate and perhaps haggle with local vendors just to get a bargained item that they can take home.

The market is located in Dong Xuan Street, Hoan Kiem District and opens daily from 6:00 AM to 7:00 PM.

6. One – Pillar Pagoda

The One – Pillar Pagoda has one of the most unique styles of architecture in Southeast Asia because the temple is shaped like a lotus flower rising from the water. It was built under the reign of Emperor Lý Thái Tông who ruled in 1028. According to historical records, the emperor was childless.

Chapter Six: Top 10 Tourist Spots in Hanoi

He then dreamt that he met a god who gave him a baby boy while seated on a lotus flower. The emperor eventually got married and met a peasant girl who bore him a son. As a sign of gratitude Lý Thái Tông erected a pillar in 1049 at the center of a lotus pond similar to the one he saw in his dream.

The temple is one of the most historical and longest cultural relics in Vietnam and it is also one of the most important structures in Hanoi. It is built out of wood on a single stone pillar that measures around 1.25 meters in diameter. One Pillar Pagoda has a square structure located on a stone pillar just like how a lotus flower would look like if it was rising from the lake. The temple is not that large but it stood through time in all its glory. It is free for visitors and opens every day from 8:00 AM to 5:00 PM.

7. *Vietnam Museum of Ethnology*

Another tourist spot that locals also love is the Vietnam Museum of Ethnology. Even those who are not so much into history will get to learn the culture and way of living of 54 ethnic minorities in the country. The museum also houses the ethnic groups' store materials such as farm tools and fishing gear as well as objects they use for everyday living such clothing, household appliances, jewelry and musical instruments.

It also contains 15,000 artifacts and over 40,000 colored photos of the different tribes. You'll also get to learn their customs, habits and culture from their religious and wedding beliefs to what kind of food they eat and the social and spiritual activities they do. If you are keen to learn the different ethnic culture in Vietnam, then head on over to this place for just 40,000 VND (around $1.50). It's open every day from 8:30 Am to 5:30 PM except on Mondays.

8. The Imperial Citadel of Thang Long

Another attraction in the Ba Dinh District is the Imperial Citadel of Thang Long. It is located at the heart of the city and it is one of the remarkable spots of interest not just for tourists in Hanoi but also for other locals in the

Chapter Six: Top 10 Tourist Spots in Hanoi

country. It is included in the UNESCO World Heritage Site in 2010 and it is also included in ten of the special national heritage treasure sites in the country. You can see various artifacts that dates back many centuries ago like old palaces, wells, ponds etc. In fact, there are many artifacts excavated in 2004 that dates back to the 6th century.

This historical site covers around18,000ha and other landmarks in clude the Hau Lau (Princess Pagoda), Bac Mon (North Gate), Kinh Thien Foundation, Doan Mon (South Gate), and Ky Dai (Flag tower). The Ky Dai is one of the oldest structure in the citadel and also has a magnificent architecture that's perfect for a photo – op. The entrance fee costs 30,000 VND and it is open daily except on Mondays from 8:00 AM to 5:00 PM.

Chapter Six: Top 10 Tourist Spots in Hanoi

9. Bat Trang Pottery Village

Bat Trang is the oldest traditional ceramic village in the city that dates back to the 7th century. It's an interesting place that will make you learn how ceramic products such as cup, pots, bottle, and bows are made and designed. You can also buy some of the finish products as a souvenir, or if you want, you can also mold one yourself and bring it back home. The shopkeeper will provide you the clay and rotating table for a fee, and also guide you on how to create and shape/ decorate your handmade ceramic product.

Chapter Six: Top 10 Tourist Spots in Hanoi

In addition to that, you can also buy key chains, bracelets, piggy banks, necklaces and other goodies.

Many tourists also had the chance to ride a vehicle being pulled by the buffalo on the way to Bat Trang Pottery Village. Since the village is located in the Gia Lam District which is quite far from the city – center, you can take the bus 47 (Long Bien – Bat Trang route) to reach the place. The bus station is just near the Dong Xuan market. If you're quite adventurous, you can rent a motorbike and go there yourself; it'll just take around 40 minutes to reach the village from the city – center.

Chapter Six: Top 10 Tourist Spots in Hanoi

10. *Hanoi Opera House*

If you want to just relax and have some local form of entertainment why not go to the historic Hanoi Opera House? It is located in downtown Hanoi where 5 city roads lead to. The structure has a unique architecture and it's also one of the top tourist destinations in the city. Hanoi Opera House was built by French architect for 10 years starting from 1901.

It is also the biggest theater in the whole country and it brings with it the culture, art, history and architecture during the French occupation. Theater fans will surely be delighted with the various events that take place in the

Chapter Six: Top 10 Tourist Spots in Hanoi

opera house including performances of traditional folk music, Vietnamese opera, international concerts and also ballet. Don't miss the chance of experiencing sitting outside the theater as well especially at night and just listen to the rhythm of the music coming from the building as you watch people walk by.

Chapter Seven: Top 10 Shopping Places in Hanoi

When it comes to shopping, the city is famed for its traditional night market, flashy boutiques, interesting shop – houses and international shopping malls that carry various international brands, entertainment and dining options. The best part of shopping in the city is that everything is walking distance. You can buy cool and interesting souvenirs along the narrow streets of the city especially in the Old Quarter where the historic Silver Street and Silk Street are located. From gimmicky souvenirs to cool local items such as silk gowns and traditional farming hats, Hanoi is a perfect shopping place for any tourists.

Chapter Seven: Top 10 Shopping Places in Hanoi

This chapter will provide you with top 10 shopping spots in the city that offers various items at the cheapest price!

1. *Hang Dao Street*

There are different night markets in the city but the highly recommended place by both locals and tourists is at Hang Dao which is located in the Old Quarter. The Hang Dao Street has a very spacious precinct that goes all the way to Dong Xuan – the oldest market place in the city. There are over 4,000 stalls along the streets of Hang Dao that offers

Chapter Seven: Top 10 Shopping Places in Hanoi

various goodies from clothes, accessories, shoes to souvenirs, jewelry, lacquer, and handicraft items at a very affordable price. The best part is that you can also buy tasty Vietnamese street foods such as noodles, soaked fruits, traditional Vietnamese cakes, and soups to fuel you as you continue your shopping expedition. The Hang Dao night market is only open on weekends from Friday to Sunday night. When going to the market, make sure to be vigilant and watch out for any pickpockets. Avoid wearing fancy jewelries or showing off your gadgets to prevent getting robbed. Haggle your way for the items you want to have because it's quite common for local vendors to charge higher if foreigners are buying their stuff.

Chapter Seven: Top 10 Shopping Places in Hanoi

2. *Hang Ma Street*

Hang Ma Street starts off alongside Hoan Kiem Lake and it also leads to Dong Xuan market but it's less crowded compared to Hang Dao Street. Still, it's one of the busiest streets in the Old Quarter and stalls offer various kinds of accessories and colorful stuff that you can take home as a souvenir or give to your friends. If you need decorations, lights, or lanterns for your house especially during the holidays or special occasions such as New Year, Autumn Festival or Christmas, then Hang Ma Street is the place to be. It's packed with both tourist and locals, and you'll surely

Chapter Seven: Top 10 Shopping Places in Hanoi

enjoy shopping around the area because of the colorful and bustling ambience. You can also find toys for kids and fancy items perfect for scrapbooking. There's also an option for those who want to have their photos taken for a small fee.

3. *Hang Duong Street*

Hang Duong Street is a great place if you want to buy snacks or simply have a food trip with your friends and family. You can buy a great selection of Vietnamese snacks particularly the famous O Mai which is widely purchased by tourists in Hanoi. It is an apricot that's covered in salt and sugar and has a nice fragrance that'll surely captivate you to

Chapter Seven: Top 10 Shopping Places in Hanoi

enter any store that offers it. It's a very flavorful snack although it tastes a bit sour at first. Hang Duong Street offers many unique recipes of the O Mai that has been handed down from one generation to another. Only in Hanoi can you find this amazing snack so make sure to buy one and let your taste buds savor each morsel of O Mai.

4, *Van Phuc Silk Village*

Van Phuc Silk Village is quite far from the city-center but it's worth the trip because you will feel like stepping back in time as it is filled with century old trees, rocky roads, and old communal houses that was quite

Chapter Seven: Top 10 Shopping Places in Hanoi

popular in the country decade ago. In addition to its preserved landscapes, the village is a paradise for shoppers looking to find the best silk. It is a place famous for the production of silk that's also being imported around the world. The silk is made by local and skilled weavers in Van Phuc, and it first made its mark in the world market back in 1931. French people love it back then which is why it became a center of silk trade both on a national and worldwide level. Every year thousands of tourists and locals shop here to find the best quality of silk.

    If you want to find the most authentic products, you should go to the prestigious shops in the village. The genuine silk is thin, tender and soft. It's very comfortable and smooth once you try it on. Chinese silk products are also available but may not be as good as the original Vietnamese handmade silk. You can bargain for a silk but keep in mind that the higher price you pay, the better its quality.

Chapter Seven: Top 10 Shopping Places in Hanoi

5. Bat Trang Pottery Village

If you are into pottery, then head on over to Bat Trang Pottery Village which is also a famous tourist attraction in Hanoi; it is located in the suburbs near the Hong River.

As mentioned in the previous chapter, it is famous for beautiful and decorated ceramic pieces that you can use as an ornament in your home. There are many striking and eye – catching designs that are also a perfect souvenir or gift. You can also be entertained as you watch skillful pottery - makers mold vases, cups, tea sets, and ceramic bowls. In addition to that, you can also learn how to make one on your

Chapter Seven: Top 10 Shopping Places in Hanoi

own by joining a workshop. It's always best to bargain for a cheaper price especially if you're going to buy cute ceramic pieces in bulk as a souvenir.

6. *Parkson Shopping Center*

Parkson Shopping Center has three main facades facing three main streets of Hanoi including Tay Son, Chua Boc and Thai Ha. You can find over a hundred stalls that sell high – end products and carry merchandise from international brands such as Guess, Tommy Hilfiger, Geox, Saint Laurent, Calvin Klein and Aigner to name a few. It's a haven for shopaholics or for those tourists who may want to splurge a bit. You will surely find the Vietnamese staff approachable and you can ask them for assistance if you are looking for something in particular. Most of them are quite fluent in English since they are usually serving foreigners.

7. Vincom Megamall Royal City

The Vincom Megamall Royal City is one of the largest underground shopping malls in all of Asia. Shop 'til you drop and prevent yourself from getting lost in a sea of

Chapter Seven: Top 10 Shopping Places in Hanoi

boutiques and stalls by getting a map – yes, it's that big! Get ready for a long day of shopping as Vincom will surely give you a feast of everything from personal items to household appliances and furniture. There's everyone for the whole family from high – end fashion clothing to the latest technological products and digital accessories. In addition to all the boutiques and stalls, you can also eat your heart out at the many international and Vietnamese restaurants that serve delectable dishes and traditionally – inspired cuisines to fuel you for more shopping extravaganza. The Vincom Megamall Royal City is located at 72A Nguyen Trai Street.

Chapter Seven: Top 10 Shopping Places in Hanoi

8. Hang Be Market

Hang Be Market is one of the most popular shopping places of Hanoians. It is located near the Hoan Kiem Lake which could be another great shopping spot for you to find various items at a cheap price if you haven't done so in other markets nearby. Expect to find flocks of locals looking to buy bulk items at a discounted price for reselling purposes. In addition to the souvenirs and fashionable clothing, Hang Be market is also famous for its line of great local cuisine, from popular street foods to delectable Vietnamese dishes. You may also notice that Hang Be Market is a great spot for

Chapter Seven: Top 10 Shopping Places in Hanoi

cultural exchange due to the many groups of international tourists and expats strolling around and shopping for cheap items the market.

9. *Hang Da Market*

Situated at the heart center of Hoan Kiem District, Hang Da market is more famous for its specialty dishes and unique food offerings. In addition to the savory and flavorful dishes being served, you can also shop for different jewelry designs, fashionable clothing and accessories for personal use and household items.

Chapter Seven: Top 10 Shopping Places in Hanoi

There is a place where you can go to that has 3 floors filled with stalls and kiosks selling different products and souvenir items which you can bargain for a discount.

10. Tet Market

Last but definitely not the least is the historic Tet Market. It's one of the largest in the city and has also become an iconic place in all of Vietnam because it has witness many battles back in the day and have stood the test of time. It's described by tourists and locals as the best wholesaler in the whole country. Needless to say, the more you buy the

Chapter Seven: Top 10 Shopping Places in Hanoi

cheaper it gets. The Tet Market offers mind – blowing diversity of products from shoes, clothes, accessories, bags, snacks, souvenirs, handicrafts, household items and other local specialties. Even if you are not fond of shopping, it's a great place to go window shopping because people here haggle all they want. You'll definitely get to see a glimpse of the Vietnamese lifestyle.

Chapter Seven: Top 10 Shopping Places in Hanoi

Chapter Eight: Top 10 Museums in Hanoi

The city of Hanoi witnessed so many historical events that shaped the metropolis we now see today. Several years of battles, invasions, sieges, and cultural changes have taken place the last centuries that also had a huge impact not just in the city but also in the entire country. If you are a history buff or you're interested in knowing more about Hanoi and how it came to be, then head on over to the many museums that are located within the city and the vicinity. Museums are the place where history is most celebrated and it's also great way for you as a tourist to get more connected to the Vietnamese culture and way of living.

Chapter Eight: Top 10 Museums in Hanoi

In this chapter, we enlisted the ten best museums in Hanoi that even those who aren't history buffs will surely appreciate

1. Air Force Museum

For those who are fans of aviation, one of the best museums and historical site in the city is the Vietnam People's Air Force Museum (Bao Tàng Phòng Không – Không Quân). It is located in the city's Bach Mai District specifically at the endpoint of the Bach Mai Airfield on Truong Chinh Street. During the Second Indochina War, the

Chapter Eight: Top 10 Museums in Hanoi

air force army of Vietnam used the Bach Mai Airfield as the control center and air defense command station.

The area which was in close proximity to the city – center and the Bach Mai Hospital was restricted and therefore untouched by the U.S. Forces during the "Rolling Thunder" Operation. As a result, the control and command of the North Vietnamese forces were unmolested. However, on November of 1967, the F-105 Thunderchiefs of the 388th Fighter Wing got a presidential approval to attack the airfield which is why bombing restrictions were eventually lifted. On May of 1972, the airfield was bombed during the Operation Linebacker I and later that year, during Operation Linebacker II, bombs were dropped in the airfield with the Bach Mai Hospital as collateral damage.

It's a pretty historic place so make sure to visit the Air Force Museum.

The entrance fee is 20,000 VND and it is open every day from 8:00 AM to 4:30 PM except on Fridays.

Location: No.173C Truong Chinh Road, Thanh Xuan District, Hanoi

Chapter Eight: Top 10 Museums in Hanoi

2. *Hoa Lo Prison Museum*

Another historic site and a thought – provoking museum for tourists is the Hoa Lo Prison Museum. It is indeed the remains of the Hoa Lo Prison, and as a matter of fact this is where the late U.S. Senator John McCain was imprisoned during the Vietnam War. The Hoa Lo Prison was ironically nicknamed as "Hanoi Hilton" by Americans who were captured, but staying there was no picnic because it was overcrowded with over 2,000 captives in 1954 even if the maximum capacity is only 600. The complex was originally built in 1896 by the French and it is only intended to house 450 inmates. The former prison house will surely

Chapter Eight: Top 10 Museums in Hanoi

pique your interest and the sculptures of inmates in each cell will remind you of the struggles they went through during those dark days of their lives.

The Hoa Lo Prison Museum is open every day from 8:00 AM to 5:00 PM for only 30,000 VND per pax.

Location: No. 1, Hoa Lo Street, Tran Hung Dao Ward, Hoan Kiem District, Hanoi City

Chapter Eight: Top 10 Museums in Hanoi

3. *Vietnamese Women's Museum*

Another top tourist attraction in the city according to the National Tourism Department is the Vietnamese Women's Museum. If you are interested about the cultural features of how women are celebrated in Vietnam or you simply want to gain insightful knowledge about feminism in the country, then head on over to the top 1 museum in the city during the ranking of the best tourist destinations of 2016. The Vietnamese Women Museum is also included in the top 25 interesting museums in Asia by TripAdvisor.

Chapter Eight: Top 10 Museums in Hanoi

There is also a free audio guide (available in French, Vietnamese and English) to aid you during your visit.

It costs 30,000 VND per person, and it is free of charge for guests who are students or have special disabilities. It is open every day from 8:00 AM to 5:00 PM.

Location: No. 36 Ly Thuong Kiet Street, Ha Noi

4. *Ho Chi Minh Museum*

The Ho Chi Minh Museum is another historical site that opened in 1990 to commemorate the anniversary of the

Chapter Eight: Top 10 Museums in Hanoi

birth of Ho Chi Minh, one of Vietnam's heroes. The museum is a Soviet – styled hagiography and one of the most informative museums in the city and in the entire country as well. It is located within the Ho Chi Minh Complex, and you'll get to know more about another famous attraction called the Ho Chi Minh Mausoleum if you come here.

In addition to the mausoleum, you'll get to see various miniatures, artifacts, and elaborate description of Ho Chi Minh's life. You'll also get to see various international and national gifts collected over the years. There are French and English descriptions of each artifact and you can also request for guided tours. The museum is open every day from 8:00 AM to 4:30PM except on Mondays for just 10,000 VND per person.

Location: No. 19, Ngoc Ha Street, Doi Can Ward, Ba Dinh District, Hanoi

Chapter Eight: Top 10 Museums in Hanoi

5. *Vietnam's Fine Arts Museum*

If you are an artsy person and history bores you, then head on over to Vietnam Fine Arts Museum. You will surely get inspired with the many contemporary and historic artworks created by Vietnamese artists over the centuries. This place will surely ignite your artistic passion and will also make you learn about the wonderful history of the country through various paintings, artifacts and other historical materials. It is indeed a promising place that even kids will enjoy!

It is opened every day from 8:30 AM to 5:00 PM for only 40,000 VND for adults and 10,000 VND for children/

teens (aged 6 to 16 years old). Children under 6 years old are free and those who are students have a discount. You can also avail a guided tour for only 150,000 VND.

Location: 66 Nguyen Thai Hoc, Ba Dinh, Ha Noi

6. *Hanoi Museum*

One of the modern museums in the city is the Hanoi Museum. If you want to know more about the Hanoians' way of living, architecture, customs and traditions in the most artistic, creative and interactive way then Hanoi

Chapter Eight: Top 10 Museums in Hanoi

Museum will surely not disappoint. Millennials and artsy tourists as well as history buffs come here to get more in – depth knowledge about the "Paris of the East." The museum's building was also included among the top beautiful architecture in Asia. The best part is that you can come here for free! It is open daily from 8:00 AM to 5:00 PM.

Location: Pham Hung Road, Nam Tu Liem District, Hanoi

7. Vietnam National Museum of History

Other museums may have already overwhelmed you with war histories and propagandas, but thanks to the superb collection and great ambience of this museum, it will come as a welcome relief. The Vietnam National Museum of History will provide you with one of the best accounts of the country's significant historical events including its modern history, culture and architecture. It's a great place to learn everything about Vietnam especially if you brought along young children with you.

Chapter Eight: Top 10 Museums in Hanoi

It is open daily from 8:00 AM to 5:00 AM except on every first Monday of each month. The entrance fee for adults cost 40,000 VND while children under 6 years of age are free of admission. There is a 50% discount for senior citizens, people with disabilities as well as veterans.

Location: No. 1, Trang Tien Street – No. 25, Tong Dan Street, Hoan Kiem District, Hanoi

Chapter Eight: Top 10 Museums in Hanoi

8. *B – 52 Victory Museum*

If you are not yet fed up with military history, then this place is another addition to the best war – related museums you can visit in the city.

The B – 52 Victory Museum commemorates the military victories of Vietnamese Forces over the years. You will learn about how Vietnamese soldiers fiercely fought for freedom, and how they defended their nation with courage and persistence for their fellow countrymen. The most prominent piece of history you need to see within the museum is the wreckage of B – 52 aircraft that's about 48,000

Chapter Eight: Top 10 Museums in Hanoi

meter in size with a wingspan of 56 meters. It is placed on an outdoor exhibit along with other aircraft debris from the Vietnam War against the United States.

Admission is free and it is open every day except on Mondays and Fridays from 8:00 AM to 4:30 PM.

Location: No.28A Dien Bien Phu Road, Ba Dinh District, Hanoi

Chapter Eight: Top 10 Museums in Hanoi

9. *Museum of People's Public Security*

The Museum of People's Public Security, also known as the Hanoi Police Museum, is another interesting museum in the city where you can learn about the heroic tradition of the country's public security officers. There are several exhibits that you can go to as well as photos you can check out that will surely pique your interest. You can see the development phases of the Socialist Republic of Vietnam and see a glimpse of what went down during the Indochina wars as well as foreign intelligence operating in the country during the 80s. You'll surely feel like you are inside a detective's room because of the many evidences and photos

Chapter Eight: Top 10 Museums in Hanoi

recorded that involve security measures done for the country.

Admission is free and it is open daily from 8:00 AM to 4:30 AM except on Sundays and Mondays.

Location: No.1 Tran Binh Trong Street, Hoan Kiem District, Hanoi

Chapter Eight: Top 10 Museums in Hanoi

10. Vietnam Military History Museum

The Vietnam Military History Museum is also known as the Army Museum and it houses various collections of weapons used throughout the country's war – filled past. History buffs and those who are interested in learning more about Vietnam will surely enjoy seeing the collections of actual weapons and war relics found during the many battles and wars against the American and French armies. You will also get to see detailed accounts of veterans who fought during the wars as well as wreckage of aircrafts,

Chapter Eight: Top 10 Museums in Hanoi

military tanks, and self – propelled guns used to conquer the gates of the Presidential Palace in Saigon that marked the end of the Vietnam War in 1975.

You can also find improvised weapons, various artifacts that date back to around 2800 B.C. during the Hong Bang Dynasty as well as classic propaganda videos and other battle exhibits.

The admission fee is 40,000 VND per person, and it is open every day from 8:00 AM to 4:30 AM except on Mondays and Fridays.

Location: No.28A Dien Bien Phu Road, Ba Dinh District, Hanoi

Chapter Eight: Top 10 Museums in Hanoi

Chapter Nine: Top 10 Nightlife Destinations in Hanoi

Hanoi's bustling streets along with great food, live entertainment and the serene sight of the Hoan Kiem Lake at night will make your evening a memorable one. Whether you'd want to spend time watching a play and a classy show, or dance and drink to your heart's content at nightclubs and bars, the city of Hanoi has plenty of places to offer. You don't have to worry anything about buying stylish clothing, although the locals will surely appreciate

Chapter Nine: Top 10 Nightlife Destinations in Hanoi

you for trying especially if you are going to see a show in their legendary theaters.

The "city of the soaring dragon" offers various activities that you can do at night by yourself or with your family and companions. You can choose to unwind by going to various live shows, watching classy performances from local and international artists, or strolling along venues and parks for that perfect photo – op.

If you're the party – goer type, Hanoi is also filled with clubs and bars that have its own theme and sound. Enjoy the local scene at night by eating street food, or just basked in the tranquility of the Hoan Kiem Lake nearby to relax you amidst the fervent action of the city. In this chapter, we've listed all the fun and cool things you can do to enjoy the night life in Hanoi.

Chapter Nine: Top 10 Nightlife Destinations in Hanoi

1. Water Puppet Show

One of the best things to do at night is to see the famous water puppet show at the Thang Long Theater. The water puppet show is one of the traditions in the country that dates back to the 11th century. During those days, the puppeteers are farmers, and they are the ones who created skits to entertain themselves. They use puppets and hid behind a bamboo screen while they are standing in the flooded rice paddies. Such entertainment was carried today but this time, the shows take place in a pool instead of

Chapter Nine: Top 10 Nightlife Destinations in Hanoi

flooded rice paddies and the puppeteers still project the puppets behind the screen so that it will appear as if it was floating over the water.

The water puppet show in Hanoi attracts tourists from all over the world, and while there are similar shows in other Vietnamese cities, Hanoi is the home of this art form. The program lasts for about an hour and contains more than 15 short skits. The show features stories that include small – town life scenes, the harvesting season, Buddhist mythology, and how King Le received a magical sword in the Hoan Kiem Lake.

The first showing starts at 3 PM followed almost every hour. Make sure to get tickets in advance from legit vendors because it almost always sells out fast due to its popularity especially among foreign visitors. Admission fee is approximately 100,000 dong per person.

Chapter Nine: Top 10 Nightlife Destinations in Hanoi

2. *Hanoi Opera House*

If you can't get enough of theater shows, then make sure to stop by at the Hanoi Opera House. In addition to being one of the best places to go to in the city especially at night, you can also enjoy seeing various artistic performances from local and international artists including opera, musicals, modern dance, and ballet. Make sure to book a ticket in advance via their website (www.hanoioperahouse.org.vn) for details on their upcoming shows and don't be surprise if the rates are quite

Chapter Nine: Top 10 Nightlife Destinations in Hanoi

high since it will depend on the kind of show you will be watching.

Don't worry though because your visit here is definitely. You will surely be entertained and you will also get to see the beautiful interior of the building. One of the best shows to consider is the Lang Toi performance which is a combination of classical Vietnamese music, acrobat, stories and contortionists.

If you don't want to see any show, we still highly recommend you to come to the Opera House and stroll alongside the building because it's beautifully lit up at night plus you'll also see elegantly dressed ladies and gentlemen attending classy shows. Definitely Instagram – worthy!

Chapter Nine: Top 10 Nightlife Destinations in Hanoi

3. Local Street Food in Hanoi

Just because it's getting late doesn't mean you can't stroll around the streets of Hanoi and taste its local street food. You will see various food stalls at night that offer delicious Vietnamese dishes which foreigners love to try. Many more local restaurants, clubs and bars are popping up on each streets to fill hungry stomachs but if you don't know where to start, then it's best to find street food vendors or dining spots that attract large Vietnamese crowds because this way you can be quite certain that the food is good and authentic.

Chapter Nine: Top 10 Nightlife Destinations in Hanoi

We recommend you to start or end your food trip in the city at the Cat Linh Dong Da which is also known as the "Barbeque Street." This is where you can find many restaurants that specializes different barbecued dishes but you'll definitely have a hard time choosing one because most of them offer the freshest and juiciest Vietnamese – style barbecues.

4. *Minh's Jazz Club*

If you want to experience local entertainment particularly good music, then make sure to stop by at Minh's Jazz Club. This is where you can find Hanoi's finest jazz musicians and jam with the latest performers in both local

Chapter Nine: Top 10 Nightlife Destinations in Hanoi

and international music scene. The dark interior of the club draws the attention of the crowd to the talented musicians on stage. In addition to live music entertainment, you may also see Minh, regarded as one of the best Vietnamese jazz performer in history, jamming with his band. Drinks are quite expensive but the live entertainment you will get is more than worthy of the price you pay.

The club is open daily from 8 PM to 12:00 midnight. It is located in Trang Tien Street, French Quarter, Hoan Kiem District.

Chapter Nine: Top 10 Nightlife Destinations in Hanoi

5. The Bank Hanoi

The Bank Hanoi is currently the largest night club in the city. It has three large venues that play different upbeat music non – stop! You can also enjoy the amazing night view of the Hoan Kiem Lake as well as downtown Hanoi because the club is located on the 6th floor of Hanoi's Capital Building. The Bank Hanoi attracts many foreign tourists, locals as well as expats who are ready to dance their heart out and party all night. There is music for everyone as their playlist include hip – hop songs, lounge music, deep house, top 40 hits as well as house tunes. The best part is that compare to other lit nightclubs in the city, drinks are not that expensive.

Chapter Nine: Top 10 Nightlife Destinations in Hanoi

Cocktails cost anywhere between 100,000 VND and 200,000 VND. International beers like Corona and Budweiser may cost you around 120,000 VND. It is open daily from 8 PM to 12:45 midnight.

6. *Hanoi Press Club*

Another great upscale bar that you should try is the Hanoi Press Club. This place offers excellent service, has a classy ambience and also has a gentleman club – styled bar. You can find excellent cocktails, wines, and delicious bar snacks while listening to live music. They also have a large

Chapter Nine: Top 10 Nightlife Destinations in Hanoi

terrace on the third floor where you can hang out with your date or have some private time. The live music only plays from Thursday to Sunday but they are open daily from 11:00 PM to 3 AM (sometimes until 5 AM). It is located in Ly Thai To Street, Hoan Kiem District. Every Thursday, they have a promo of buy – one – get – one drink on selected liquors.

7. *The Vietnam Central Circus*

This is a great place to go to especially if you brought your family with you. Visitors can enjoy live performances

Chapter Nine: Top 10 Nightlife Destinations in Hanoi

as well as fairground games for children. It is held at the southern area of Hanoi within a large park and it also features animal performances, magic and acrobatic show. Since it is just right next to the Thien Quang Lake, you can just walk there if you're coming from the Old Quarter. The Central Circus follows a predictable program but it sure is worthy of your time. It is open from Tuesday to Sunday at 8:00 PM to 10:00 PM. The location is Tran Nhan Tong, Nguyen Du, Hai Ba Trung, Hanoi.

Chapter Nine: Top 10 Nightlife Destinations in Hanoi

8. The Legend Beer

Legend Beer is a 3 – story bar that has a nice terrace overlooking Hoan Kiem Lake and downtown Hanoi. According to locals and foreign visitors, there's no better bar in Hanoi that offers the best ice cold beer while sightseeing the night time escapades of the city's inhabitants. Since the terrace is quite low level, you can feel that you are part of the fervent action of the busy street down below. It is both entertaining to watch and relaxing at the same time. You can also taste their own brewed drinks with dark stout, wheat beer and lager that are available in several sizes.

Chapter Nine: Top 10 Nightlife Destinations in Hanoi

It's also best to taste their sausages and pork knuckle dishes served in German – style along with your chosen drink. The Legend Beer is open daily from 10:00 PM to 5AM and it is located at Dinh Tien Hoang, Hanoi.

9. *Dragonfly Bar and Lounge*

One of the longstanding bars in the city is the Dragonfly Bar and Lounge. It is located in the Old Quarter and attracts young locals and expats as well. If you are in your 20s, this is the best place for you to hang out with your fellow millennials. They have hip – hop and pop music that young

Chapter Nine: Top 10 Nightlife Destinations in Hanoi

professionals dance to all night so if you want to get in the groove, you can do so in their spacious dance area. If you prefer to just mix and mingle, or talk to the locals, you can have that over the bar's popular cocktail offerings at a relatively affordable price. Head upstairs to enjoy a shisha pipe that's available in various flavors. The Dragonfly Bar and Lounge is open daily from 8:00 PM to 12 midnight and it is located at Hang Buom, Hoan Kiem District.

10. Sunset Bar

If you want to splurge and hang out with affluent locals and tourists, the Sunset Bar is within the InterContinental Hotel is the night spot for you. It is located at the West Lake in the Tay Ho District where you can enjoy

Chapter Nine: Top 10 Nightlife Destinations in Hanoi

a cool and relaxed evening since it is far away from the hustle and bustle of the city – center.

You'll surely enjoy the bar's great cocktails and interior as well as the serene view of the lake. Sunset Bar is accessible via the torch – lit bridge if you're coming from the InterContinental Hotel; walking on the bridge is also a great photo – op that's Instagram – worthy. Guests can also relax on the comfortable couches on the wooden deck of the bar while enjoying premium wines and signature drinks. It is open daily from 4:30 PM to 12 midnight.

Chapter Nine: Top 10 Nightlife Destinations in Hanoi

Chapter Ten: Off - Beaten Path in Hanoi

Hanoi is a buzzing metropolis that's unlike any other city in Southeast Asia, and perhaps in the world. The *Paris of the East* is home to the longest - running communist government in the world which could be an unknown fact for most of you. Every year foreigners flock here to soak in the Asian ambience, see historical sites, eat flavorful Vietnamese dishes, enjoy the vibrant nightlife and get lost in its hustle and bustle. There are many things to do in the city but most tourists are inclined to stick to the "top 10 lists," and though it is true that no visit to Hanoi is complete

Chapter Ten: Off - Beaten Path in Hanoi

without checking out historical sites such as the Hoan Kiem Lake and the Ho Chi Minh Park, there are still many things to see and experience that can make this trip more meaningful and memorable. In this chapter, we have enlisted top ten off – the – beaten paths that you can visit. Get ready to experience the other side of Hanoi and have that wanderlust moment for yourself!

1. *Propaganda Posters*

As we've mentioned earlier, Hanoi is the home of the longest – running communist government in the world, and like all totalitarian regimes, state propagandas and artworks

Chapter Ten: Off - Beaten Path in Hanoi

that were officially sanctioned have played an important role in reaching the locals and imparting the message of political parties especially during the Vietnam War. You can go around the city and find many propaganda posters in the government buildings to see if for yourself. If you want to check out vintage collections of propaganda artworks such as images of burning the aircrafts of U.S. Forces and other similar messages, you can find them in special galleries located in the Old Quarter. You can also buy a couple of them as they make cool souvenirs.

2. 54 Traditions Gallery

Another great artsy place that will surely pique your interest is the 54 Traditions Gallery. The place is quite cluttered because it is packed with antiquities, captivating artworks and other cool objects that are made by Vietnamese ethnic groups who were craftsmen. Like much of the world, the country is also becoming more centralized and modern which is why it's easy to forget about the rich cultural diversity that still exists especially in the villages when you are in the city – center. This is why it's quite refreshing to see a glimpse of Vietnam's ancient beliefs, customs and

Chapter Ten: Off - Beaten Path in Hanoi

traditions through the arts and craft produce by the natives. You will see agricultural tools, wooden statues, and other ethnic items that you can buy as a souvenir. Be careful though because you may buy an item that could have "shamanic curse" for which the gallery doesn't have any liability. If you don't want to risk being unlucky or being cursed, then we suggest you just check it out and get a guided tour for free. It is located at Hang Bun which is just a few minutes away from the Old Quarter.

Chapter Ten: Off - Beaten Path in Hanoi

3. Heritage Walk

As the sun sets, you will see how Hanoi transforms at night in a whole new way. The restaurants and clubs attract guests with their neon lights, the landmarks and monuments lit up, the ambience become more refreshing and take on a different air than during the day. We highly recommend you to see the city from a new perspective by strolling at night and walk past your favorite spots one more time after dark as it will be quite a different experience. You will see Hanoi come to life especially when you head to the Old Quarter where iconic hotels and landmarks lit up their facades. Take your time as you do this heritage walk because you'll surely notice many things you haven't seen during the day. Take in all the hidden details of Hanoi and you will see something that more than meets the eye.

4. Art Scene

If you are an artsy type of person and you're not fond of going to clubs, shows or hanging out in bars, you can check out the lively art scene of the city. Hanoi boasts its

Chapter Ten: Off - Beaten Path in Hanoi

eclectic mix of artists and artworks that you will surely appreciate. Local artists come to the city to promote their craft, meet fellow artists, and connect with tourists as well. You can check out latest projects through an exhibit while you're mingling with other people over some drinks. We recommend you to go to Manzi which is an art gallery located at Phan Huy Ich because they offer a nice spot for creative people to mingle with one another and feature many contemporary artworks.

Chapter Ten: Off - Beaten Path in Hanoi

5. The Landmark 72

Due to the old structure of the city, there aren't many tall buildings around. Luckily, there is one called the Landmark 72 which is also the tallest tower not just in Hanoi but in the entire country. It is located in the financial district at Phan Hung Boulevard where tourists can visit and have a nice panoramic view of the city. It is a 70 – storey building standing at about 1,100 feet and it is home to the offices of many local and international companies as well as a 5 – star hotel. Visitors will surely enjoy Hanoi's skyline especially at night, and you can also head to the hotel lounge afterwards

Chapter Ten: Off - Beaten Path in Hanoi

for a drink or two. There is also a so – called "stair race" that happens annually where players race up the 1,914 steps of the building! If you happen to be there during the stair race then you're in for an awesome experience!

6. *Vietnamese Museum of Revolution*

If you want to learn and better understand the contemporary Vietnamese society then this place is a must – see! Don't let the outer appeal of the place put you off as it can be quite fascinating especially if you love war stories.

Chapter Ten: Off - Beaten Path in Hanoi

The museum exhibits the country's struggle for independence from 1858 to 1945, the War of Resistance from 1945 to 1975 and the country's road to recovery. You can also check out cool exhibits of old photos and letters from the many battles of Vietnam as well as the iron shackles used by Americans who were imprisoned back then, bullets, bomb remains and other wreckages. The museum is located at the Tong Dan district where it's not that crowded with tourists. You might want to take a rickshaw to its gates to avoid getting lost.

7. *Bridegroom Field*

The Bridegroom field is a great place for you to relax after strolling around the city and have some quiet time away from the crowd. The reason why this area is name as such is because this is where wedding photographers usually take their clients to pose for their pre – nuptials since it's one of the few tranquil spots in Hanoi that's just a short distance from the fervent action of the city. The Bridegroom field is located near the Red River and it's also the closest thing to being in the countryside without actually heading to countryside.

Chapter Ten: Off - Beaten Path in Hanoi

It's also a nice place where you can just hang out and watch the sun go down while seeing the happy faces of the pre – weds as they smile for the camera. If you're coming from the Old Quarter, it's best to ride a motorbike to reach the North Dyke road where the field is located.

Chapter Ten: Off - Beaten Path in Hanoi

8. The Bookworm

The Bookworm believe it or not is the city's (and perhaps the country's) leading English language bookshop. You'll find tons of new books and you can also find tomes that are available for purchase and your perusal. Like other bookshops, the Bookworm also has a café bar where they serve Vietnamese coffee. It's a great place to read books and also meet other tourists who can speak English. The

Chapter Ten: Off - Beaten Path in Hanoi

Bookworm is one of the simplest places that offer a cultural exchange in the city. They also host readings from local authors every now and then so make sure to check out their website if you want to catch these events while you're in town. The book store is located just a few blocks from the Ho Truch Bach Lake in Chau Long area. It's best to take a cab if you're coming from the Old Quarter.

Chapter Ten: Off - Beaten Path in Hanoi

9. Kien Hung Commune

If you want to do something cool, say making your own knife, then head on over to the Kien Hung Commune! In today's modern and tech – savvy world, it's sometimes nice to just take a step back and do things the old – fashioned way. Making your own knife at the blacksmith's workshop located in Ha Dong Town is a great place to go back to basics. You can watch how kitchen utensils and Vietnamese cooking woks are made in the traditional way. If you're up for it, you can also join a knife – making course where under the guidance of an expert specifically a master blacksmith, you can create and customize your own knife.

Chapter Ten: Off - Beaten Path in Hanoi

You'll learn how to form a handle, how to sharpen and shape the blade, and also do some testing if your finished output can slice up a mango! Perhaps the only downside is that Ha Dong Town is not connected to the central transport network of Hanoi which means you need to walk to Tang Trien area to catch a bus and travel for about an hour before you get there but it sure is worth the trip!

10. *Vietnam National Museum of Nature*

If you're more of an environmentalist, or you simply love nature then why not visit the Vietnam National Museum of

Chapter Ten: Off - Beaten Path in Hanoi

Nature. It is a leading museum that showcases the basic features of the country's nature and environment. You can find lots of exhibits about how the country preserves its natural resources and information about local plants and the like. It is located inside the campus of Vietnam Academy of Science and Technology at the Cau Giay district. Many tourists also visit this place despite of its relatively small exhibits because of its nice interior and design. You can see specimens encased in glasses as well as models placed outside. Pets are allowed for weekend outdoors. It is open from Thursday to Sunday, 8:30 AM to 4:30 PM. The admission fee is just 20,000 VND per person.

Quick Travel Guide

The rule in Hanoi is simple: walk an even pace, get eye contact and don't panic! As soon as you first cross the streets of Hanoi, you may think that it is a life or death situation but behind all the madness, you'll soon learn how to go with the flow and be one with the city. The subtle beauty of Hanoi will soon be noticeable to you as you discover the best spots and experience the city's essence. From the amazing flavors found at the countless street vendors to its vibrant and historical sites, Hanoi is all about seeing, hearing and tasting what it has to offer.

We hope you have a great time traversing the busy streets of the city and find hidden gems within. It's always best to leave your expectations behind, let your curiosity flow and just immerse yourself in one of the most fascinating cities in Asia.

1. Travel Essentials

- **Currency** – Vietnamese Dong (VND)
- **Primary Language Spoken:** Vietnamese, French, English
- **Exchange Rate:** As of this writing, the exchange rate is $1USD = 23,195 Vietnamese Dong (VND).
- **ATMs:** Everything in the metropolis follows a cash only basis though some high – end places may accept credit cards/ debit cards.

Electric and Voltage

- When it comes to voltage, the standard electricity voltage in the country is 220 Volts at 50Hz. You can use your devices as long as the label says that it is "50

– 60Hz" or "100 – 240 volts." It is compatible provided that you have the right plugs.

- To make your device work, you need to buy a transformer to convert the voltage and make it compatible. You can purchase adapters or converters in various convenient stores as well as bookstores. It may cost you around $4 or more.

Communication Services

- The telephone code in Hanoi is 4. However, do keep in mind that the number 3 should be added in front of the local numbers.
    o Dial 3 (+local number) from within the city, or 04 (+local number) for inter – provincial calls. Dial +84 4 (+local number) from overseas calls.

- You can find lots of internet cafes around the city. Most internet cafes are used by teenagers and you'll see them just playing online games and battle games. The rates will vary but it can start for as low as 3,000 dong per hour. You'll also find slightly high – end internet cafes in the Old Quarter where most tourists are, and they have computers that are capable of video calls and international phone calls.

Best Time to Go

- You shouldn't schedule your trip during the rainy season which is from May to September. The average temperature in the city is 23°C with a humidity of around 79%. The highest recorded temperature is around 42°C back in 1926, while the lowest is 2.7 °C back in 1955.

Do's and Don't's

- Do store your cash, tickets, credit/ debit cards as well as other valuables in a secure place.
- Do get the hotel business card from the reception desk before you go out so that it'll be easier for you to return.
- Do bring along with you a toilet paper especially if you're going to take a trip.

- Do dress appropriately especially if you're going to visit culturally sensitive areas or places of worship such as pagodas and temples.
- Do drink lots of bottle water so as not to get dehydrated especially if you visit the city during the summer.
- Do remove your shoes at the front door if you get invited to a Vietnamese household
- Do ask for permission if you're going to use the restroom and properly excuse yourself.
- Don't wear too much flashy things such as jewelries or flaunt your gadgets around so as not to attract potential robbers.
- Don't wear shorts, skirts, low – neck lines, and other revealing clothing especially when going to sacred places
- Don't give away candies, water bottles, or other plastic materials to locals especially if you find yourself trekking through minority villages because they may not know how to properly dispose it.
- Don't sleep with the feet of your soles pointing to the family altar if for instance you will be sleeping in someone else's house.

- Don't lose your temper in public to avoid trouble or lose face.
- Don't take photos of anything that has to do with the military (unless you're allowed) as it can be a breach of national security.
- Don't take videos of the ethnic groups when going to minority villages as it can be intrusive to the locals.

2. *Transportation*

Transportation Options from the Airport:

Via Taxi

- Turn to your right if you're coming from the domestic terminal, or turn left if you're landing from international terminal. All the taxis in Hanoi are run by meter, and they are provided by different cab companies.
- The estimated cost of going to the Old Quarter from the airport is 300,000 to 350,000 dong (around 28 km distance on the meter). If you're going to the French Quarter from the airport, it may cost a little more but

still less than 400,000 dong. Some drivers will ask more than 400,000 dong if they see more than 2 foreigners, but just ignore them.
- It will only take 30 to 40 minutes from the airport to Hanoi but may take a bit longer depending on the traffic.

Via Express Buses
- Bus 86 usually takes the expressway all the way up to the first stop which is the Tay Ho area followed by the Long Bien station, Opera House, Melia Hotel and Rail Station. The bus arrives every 25 minutes, and runs from 6:20 AM to 11:00 PM.
- From the international terminal, you can find the express bus at pillar 2, second road near the arrivals area. You just have to turn left after exiting the international terminal.
- If you're coming from the city – center going to the airport, express buses starts at 5:05 AM until 10:40 PM. You should go to the booth located at the south end of the main railway station.

Via Public Buses

- To catch the public buses, you need to head over to the first floor of the terminal, go outside and find the bus parking lot since this is the end stop of the bus routes.
- It'll take you around 90 minutes or more before arriving to Hanoi. You can take Bus 07 as it crosses the Thang Long Bridge and heads up to the western area of Hanoi which is about an hour away from the central area of the city. Bus 17 crosses the Chuong Duong Bridge and comes near the Old Quarter and the Hoan Kiem Lake area where most tourists stay.

Via Train

- Trains use the main station (located in Ga Hang Co) for daily services in and out of the city not just Hanoi but also Saigon, Lao Cai, Nha Trang, Hue and others.
- Tickets for all destinations in Vietnam are sold at the main station and the ticket booth is divided into two; the north and south counters which serves their respective cities.

- We highly recommend that you purchase tickets as soon as you can because some sleeper tickets can be sold out easily. If you can't buy a ticket, you can go to a travel agent and see if they still have any, or try your luck at the station just a few minutes before boarding time because some agents hold and sell it for a slightly higher price.

Transportation Options In the City:

Via Cyclo - Taxis

- Cyclo – taxis are not cars but more of a 4 to 7 – seater motorbikes. Within Hanoi, there are 3 companies that are reliable; the Taxi Group (which is Hanoi Taxi and CP Taxi) are color white, the Mai Linh which are color green, and the Taxi NoiBai but they specialize in airport transfers and not in getting around the city.
- Some drivers automatically demand 200,000 dong for just 100 meter. You can try to haggle and get tangled up with their language but if that's how you're going

to get a lower fare then consider all of that as part of the Hanoi experience.

- If you like a flat fee, it's best to use the app GrabTaxi which functions just like an Uber. You can just input your destination, agree on the price and book it. GrabTaxi drivers only accept cash as payment.

Via Motorbike Taxis

- You can choose to ride a motorbike taxi particularly if you're staying the Old Quarter since they're almost at every corner. However, don't try to find them because if they see that you do, they will try to increase the price, so show only faint interest. You should haggle and firmly agree on a fix price to avoid being ripped.
- It's best to write down the fare and get an okay from the driver – this will serve as your receipt as well. Once you get one, the driver will give you a helmet.

Via Motorbike Rental

- If you prefer driving on your own while soaking in the chaotic motorbike town of Hanoi, you can rent one for $6 to 7 per day.
- A word of caution though, we cannot emphasize how chaotic and undisciplined the drivers are in Hanoi. All of them don't follow the rules, and there are also no pedestrian lanes. Some drivers will always cut you off, and people will constantly just cross the street so make sure to be extra careful because the city is not the place to practice your motorcycle skills.
- When you're parking, make sure to lock the front wheel and park in places with other bikes. Some shops have bike attendants that'll give you a parking ticket and the fee may cost between 2,000 and 5,000 dong.

Via Bus

- There are also buses that can tour you around the city which are cheap and usually scam – free.

- Make sure to pick up the bus line map which can be found at the Trang Tien Street or by the book street near the Opera House.
- Identify the lines and the routes before going to the bus stop. Wait for the bus to arrive and pay the fare. As of this writing, it may cost you 7,000 dong.

3. Hanoi Highlights

Tourist Spots:

- Hoan Kiem Lake
- President Ho Chi Minh Mausoleum
- Old Quarter
- The Temple of Literature
- Dong Xuan Market
- The One – Pillar Pagoda
- Vietnam Museum of Ethnology
- Imperial Citadel of Thang Long
- Bat Trang Pottery Village
- Hanoi Opera House

Museums

- Air Force Museum
- Hoa Lo Prison Museum
- Vietnamese Women's Museum
- Ho Chi Minh Museum
- Vietnam's Fine Arts Museum
- Hanoi Museum
- Vietnam National Museum of History
- B - 52 Victory Museum
- Museum of People's Public Security
- Vietnam Military History Museum

Night Life and Off - the - Beaten Path

- Water Puppet Show
- Hanoi Opera House
- Minh's Jazz Club
- Vietnam National Museum of Nature
- The Vietnam Central Circus
- 54 Traditions Gallery
- The Landmark 72
- Vietnamese Museum of Revolution

Index

airport 33, 34, 35, 36, 39, 46, 48, 51, 52, 54, 56, 62, 64, 176, 177, 179

bars 5, 45, 51, 62, 136, 137, 142, 151, 160

clubs 137, 142, 159, 160

culture 3, 4, 1, 3, 5, 23, 75, 83, 89, 95, 101, 118, 129, 171

customs 18, 95, 127, 157

dishes 19, 66, 67, 72, 74, 113, 114, 115, 142, 143, 150, 154

district 6, 8, 2, 3, 14, 46, 93, 97, 100, 115, 119, 120, 122, 125, 128, 129, 131, 133, 135, 145, 148, 152

Dos and Don'ts's 28

entertainment 101, 103, 136, 138, 144

etiquette 18, 19, 20, 202

exhibits 132, 135, 164, 170

express buses 35, 36, 177

French Quarter 2, 3, 5, 34, 45, 145, 176

Hanoi 1, 3, 1, 2, 3, 4, 5, 7, 8, 9, 13, 14, 15, 16, 17, 18, 22, 24, 26, 27, 28, 33, 34, 35, 36, 37, 38, 39, 41, 42, 45, 48, 49, 50, 51, 52, 53, 54, 55, 56, 58, 59, 60, 61, 62, 63, 64, 65, 66, 69, 72, 75, 80, 82, 83, 84, 85, 86, 90, 94, 96, 97, 101, 103, 107, 110, 111, 118, 119, 120, 121, 122, 125, 127, 128, 129, 131, 132, 133, 135, 136, 137, 139, 140, 142, 144, 145, 147, 148, 149, 150, 154, 155, 159, 160, 162, 165, 169, 173, 176, 178, 179, 180, 182, 183, 194, 198, 199, 200, 201, 202, 203

hotels 5, 22, 29, 44, 45, 159, 201

internet 2, 27, 173

markets 5, 92, 104, 114

mausoleum .... 86, 87, 125 metropolis 1, 4, 5, 8, 23, 24, 33, 118, 154, 172

museums 3, 4, 25, 118, 119, 123, 125, 127, 128, 130, 200, 203

night life 3, 137

noodles 67, 69, 73, 105

off – the – beaten 155

Old Quarter .. 2, 5, 27, 34, 36, 38, 40, 44, 50, 51, 72, 79, 81, 82, 88, 89, 103, 104, 106, 148, 151, 156, 158, 159, 166, 167, 173, 176, 178, 180, 182

rates 27, 56, 140, 173

region 4, 9, 44

restaurant 46, 68, 71, 72, 73, 77, 78, 79, 80

shopping 4, 103, 104, 105, 107, 112, 114, 117, 200, 203

shows 137, 138, 139, 140, 141, 160

souvenirs 24, 92, 103, 104, 114, 117, 156

stalls 92, 104, 106, 111, 113, 116, 142

street food 5, 137, 142

taxis 34, 39, 176, 179

Tickets 37, 178

tourist spot 95

tourists 3, 4, 5, 6, 18, 27, 33, 36, 38, 45, 48, 50, 60, 66, 67, 70, 72, 78, 81, 82, 83, 84, 92, 97, 100, 103, 104, 107, 109, 112, 115, 116, 121, 128, 139, 146, 152, 154, 161, 162, 164, 167, 170, 173, 178, 203

Trains 37, 178

Vietnamese 2, 3, 5, 6, 13, 15, 17, 18, 19, 20, 21, 22, 24, 26, 29, 30, 44, 47, 51, 53, 55, 57, 63, 65, 66, 69, 74, 75, 76, 77, 80, 81, 83, 87, 90, 92, 102, 105, 107, 109, 112, 113, 114, 117, 118, 120, 123, 126, 130, 139, 141, 142, 143, 144, 154, 157, 163, 167, 168, 172, 174, 182, 183, 201

PHOTO REFERENCES

Page 1 Photo by user 9636137 via Pixabay.com, https://pixabay.com/en/tran-quoc-pagoda-old-pagoda-in-hanoi-3559145/

Page 4 Photo by user GRT via Pixabay.com, https://pixabay.com/en/hanoi-sunset-lake-city-scape-1528199/

Page 7 Photo by user Leon_Ting via Pixabay.com, https://pixabay.com/en/hanoi-vietnam-asia-tourism-599202/

Page 17 Photo by user Manhdoan via Pixabay.com, https://pixabay.com/en/long-coat-hat-dress-beauty-1531952/

Page 22 Photo by user KatherineSlade via Pixabay.com, https://pixabay.com/en/hanoi-vietnam-street-traffic-701176/

Page 33 Photo by user Leon_Ting via Pixabay.com, https://pixabay.com/en/hanoi-vietnam-city-busy-bikes-599203/

Page 44 Photo by user 9636137 via Pixabay.com, https://pixabay.com/en/hanoi-old-quarter-3559137/

Page 46 Photo by user Shawn Harquail via Flickr.com, https://www.flickr.com/photos/harquail/38633199651/

Page 48 Photo by user仁仔 何 via Flickr.com, https://www.flickr.com/photos/happykiddo4ever/19087461665/

Page 50 Photo by user Roderick Eime via Flickr.com, https://www.flickr.com/photos/rodeime/11403016403/

Page 52 Photo by user David McKelvey via Flickr.com, https://www.flickr.com/photos/dgmckelvey/9899190224/

Page 54 Photo by user Rajesh_India via Flickr.com, https://www.flickr.com/photos/pamnani/29185493457/

Page 56 Photo by user David McKelvey via Flickr.com, https://www.flickr.com/photos/dgmckelvey/16007709444/

Page 58 Photo by user S Tsui via Flickr.com, https://www.flickr.com/photos/n0r/67567669/

Page 60 Photo by user David McKelvey via Flickr.com, https://www.flickr.com/photos/dgmckelvey/16248516249/

Page 62 Photo by user Roderick Eime via Flickr.com, https://www.flickr.com/photos/rodeime/11402888154/

Page 64 Photo by user Roderick Eime via Flickr.com, https://www.flickr.com/photos/rodeime/11402870516/

Page 66 Photo by user Marco Verch via Flickr.com, https://www.flickr.com/photos/30478819@N08/35306707484/

Page 67 Photo by user Guilhem Vellut via Flickr.com, https://www.flickr.com/photos/o_0/33489861756/

Page 69 Photo by user Guilhem Vellut via Flickr.com, https://www.flickr.com/photos/o_0/33470587566/

Page 71 Photo by user Christian Scholz via Flickr.com, https://www.flickr.com/photos/mrtopf/11328443/

Page 73 Photo by user Sanderslelli via Flickr.com, https://www.flickr.com/photos/sanders_lelli/3639289596/

Page 74 Photo by user kantnews via Flickr.com, https://pixabay.com/en/coffee-egg-coffee-hanoi-delicious-3723049/

Page 76 Photo by user omnia2070 via Flickr.com, https://www.flickr.com/photos/66145957@N05/13940315649/

Page 77 Photo by user Ẩm Thực Đam Mê via Flickr.com, https://www.flickr.com/photos/148481438@N03/27613660509

Page 79 Photo by user Ẩm Thực Đam Mê via Flickr.com, https://www.flickr.com/photos/148481438@N03/37015635956

Page 80 Photo by user Ẩm Thực Đam Mê via Flickr.com, https://www.flickr.com/photos/148481438@N03/37872405402

Page 81 Photo by user Hideya Hamano via Flickr.com, https://www.flickr.com/photos/mawari/35484614015/

Page 83 Photo by user David McKelvey via Flickr.com, https://www.flickr.com/photos/dgmckelvey/16638714391/

Page 84 Photo by user Pablo Gonzalez via Flickr.com, https://www.flickr.com/photos/pablo_javier/34349639882/

Page 86 Photo by user Eugene via Flickr.com, https://www.flickr.com/photos/yoodz/8109423639/

Page 88 Photo by user Flip Nomad via Flickr.com, https://www.flickr.com/photos/flipnomad/5706545676/

Page 89 Photo by user Daniel Mennerich via Flickr.com, https://www.flickr.com/photos/danielmennerich/30592252315/

Page 91 Photo by user Khánh Hmoong via Flickr.com, https://www.flickr.com/photos/hmoong/10709174065/

Page 92 Photo by user Malingering via Flickr.com, https://www.flickr.com/photos/malingering/5677757522/

Page 94 Photo by user Daniel Mennerich via Flickr.com, https://www.flickr.com/photos/danielmennerich/32097739872/

Page 95 Photo by user Geekoftheweek via Flickr.com, https://www.flickr.com/photos/geekoftheweek/32316017423/

Page 97 Photo by user Carl Stead via Flickr.com, https://www.flickr.com/photos/cristic/6909983514/

Page 99 Photo by user Fred Sharples via Flickr.com, https://www.flickr.com/photos/ballena/2092644860/

Page 101 Photo by user Nguyen Hung Vu via Flickr.com, https://www.flickr.com/photos/vuhung/26837121521/

Page 102 Photo by user Nguyenhuynhmai via Pixabay.com, https://pixabay.com/en/fair-people-women-oranges-apples-1505686/

Page 104 Photo by user GothPhil via Flickr.com, https://www.flickr.com/photos/phil_p/45355803384/

Page 105 Photo by user Everjean via Flickr.com, https://www.flickr.com/photos/evert-jan/314292259/

Page 106 Photo by user Neville Wootton via Flickr.com, https://www.flickr.com/photos/nevillewootton/32577147803/

Page 108 Photo by user mmmmngai@rogers.com via Flickr.com, https://www.flickr.com/photos/12720221@N08/39702793614/

Page 109 Photo by user Myna Bird via Flickr.com, https://www.flickr.com/photos/myna_bird/2995114866/

Page 110 Photo by user Mr. & Mrs. Backpacker via Flickr.com, https://www.flickr.com/photos/mrandmrsbackpacker/9501838320/

Page 112 Photo by user Shankar S. via Flickr.com, https://www.flickr.com/photos/shankaronline/31417145486/in/photostream/

Page 113 Photo by user Ssedro via Flickr.com, https://www.flickr.com/photos/ssedro/4702309286/

Page 114 Photo by user Hanoi Mark via Flickr.com, https://www.flickr.com/photos/riverdaleto/108951213/

Page 116 Photo by user Chris Goldberg via Flickr.com, https://www.flickr.com/photos/chrisgold/8512326422/

Page 117 Photo by user fredsharples via Flickr.com, https://www.flickr.com/photos/ballena/2091869957/in/photolist

Page 119 Photo by user David McKelvey via Flickr.com, https://www.flickr.com/photos/dgmckelvey/7069173829/

Page 121 Photo by user Michael Coghlan via Flickr.com, https://www.flickr.com/photos/mikecogh/18580337949/

Page 122 Photo by user wolfishstein via Flickr.com, https://www.flickr.com/photos/orinoconw/5956313327/

Page 124 Photo by user Mindy McAdams via Flickr.com, https://www.flickr.com/photos/macloo/9366451018/

Page 125 Photo by user Daniel Mennerich via Flickr.com, https://www.flickr.com/photos/danielmennerich/31886836625/

Page 127 Photo by user mrgarethm via Flickr.com, https://www.flickr.com/photos/mrgarethm/14428535169/

Page 129 Photo by user Simon Morris via Flickr.com, https://www.flickr.com/photos/simonmgc/45542588632/

Page 131 Photo by user Allan Watt via Flickr.com, https://www.flickr.com/photos/130467353@N06/16565661086/

Page 133 Photo by user Holiday Point via Flickr.com, https://www.flickr.com/photos/holidaypointau/8120860644/

Page 135 Photo by user Phong Nguyen via Flickr.com, https://www.flickr.com/photos/hpweddingphoto/24741835429/

Page 137 Photo by user Isriya Paireepairit via Flickr.com, https://www.flickr.com/photos/isriya/7180126438/

Page 139 Photo by user Jason via Flickr.com, https://www.flickr.com/photos/saigonbisbee/313910632/

Page 141 Photo by user Paul Galow via Flickr.com, https://www.flickr.com/photos/edikonfetti/11516756614/

Page 142 Photo by user ctot_not_def via Flickr.com, https://www.flickr.com/photos/ctot_non_def/2460406482/

Page 144 Photo by user David McKelvey via Flickr.com, https://www.flickr.com/photos/dgmckelvey/16475002957/

Page 145 Photo by user Chris Goldberg via Flickr.com, https://www.flickr.com/photos/chrisgold/8474470999/

Page 146 Photo by user Morgaine via Flickr.com, https://www.flickr.com/photos/morgaine/3710541279/

Page 148 Photo by user Adam Wilson via Flickr.com, https://www.flickr.com/photos/adamwilson/34154758206/

Page 149 Photo by user deepwarren via Flickr.com, https://www.flickr.com/photos/fuzzhead/2895204883/

Page 150 Photo by user PC via Flickr.com, https://www.flickr.com/photos/lambretic/5131533651/

Page 152 Photo by user David McKelvey via Flickr.com, https://www.flickr.com/photos/dgmckelvey/7060653969/

Page 153 Photo by user torbakhopper via Flickr.com, https://www.flickr.com/photos/gazeronly/23947478213/

Page 155 Photo by user U.S. Army via Flickr.com, https://www.flickr.com/photos/familymwr/4929686303/

Page 157 Photo by user motlancuoi2018 via Pixabay.com, https://pixabay.com/en/vietnam-hanoi-hanoi-city-bicycle-3741412/

Page 158 Photo by user Rod Waddington via Flickr.com, https://www.flickr.com/photos/rod_waddington/31986563328/

Page 160 Photo by user manhhai via Flickr.com, https://www.flickr.com/photos/13476480@N07/29403599327/

Page 161 Photo by user STEPHEN J MASON Photography via Flickr.com, https://www.flickr.com/photos/calflier001/6869069454/

Page 163 Photo by user Mgzkun via Flickr.com, https://www.flickr.com/photos/27138197@N08/16516367497/

Page 165 Photo by user Bê Swifty via Flickr.com, https://www.flickr.com/photos/b_swifty/15718642129/

Page 167 Photo by user David McKelvey via Flickr.com, https://www.flickr.com/photos/dgmckelvey/9778646522/

Page 168 Photo by user Raymond June via Flickr.com, https://www.flickr.com/photos/raymondjune/14998589901/

Page 170 Photo by user Quangpraha via Pixabay.com, htttps://pixabay.com/en/the-ancient-village-forestry-road-3358831/

REFERENCES

Top 10 things to do when travelling to Hanoi - Unveil the hidden gems of Hanoi beauty - GoldenHolidayTravel.com

https://goldenholidaytravel.com/top-10-things-to-do-in-hanoi-that-you-should-not-miss.new

Vietnam: 10 Not So Obvious Places to Visit - TravelHappy.info

https://travelhappy.info/vietnam/vietnam-10-not-so-obvious-places-to-visit/

Hanoi - Wikipedia.org

https://en.wikipedia.org/wiki/Hanoi

Hanoi - Revolvy.com

https://www.revolvy.com/page/Hanoi

Hanoi after Dark: The Ultimate Guide to Nightlife in Hanoi - Christinas.vn

https://blog.christinas.vn/guide-to-nightlife-in-hanoi-after-dark/

Top 10 Things to Do in Hanoi at Night - TheCultureTrip.com

https://theculturetrip.com/asia/vietnam/articles/top-10-things-to-do-in-hanoi-at-night/

Hanoi - Wikivoyage.org

https://en.wikivoyage.org/wiki/Hanoi

Top 13 Fascinating Museums In Hanoi – Travellers Should Not Miss - HanoiFreeLocalTours.com

https://hanoifreelocaltours.com/museums-in-hanoi/

The Most Fascinating Museums In Hanoi, Vietnam -The Culture Trip

https://theculturetrip.com/asia/vietnam/articles/the-most-fascinating-museums-in-hanoi-vietnam/

10 Best Shopping in Hanoi: Greatest Places to Shop in Hanoi - Vietnam - Guide.com

http://www.vietnam-guide.com/hanoi/top10/top10-hanoi-shopping.htm

Top 10 Hanoi Attractions - ILoveVietnamTour.com

https://ilovevietnamtour.com/top-10-hanoi-attractions/

Top 10 Best Places To Shop In Hanoi - JustGola.com

https://www.justgola.com/blog/top-10-best-places-to-shop-in-hanoi-75

20 Must-Visit Attractions in Hanoi - The Culture Trip

https://theculturetrip.com/asia/vietnam/articles/20-must-visit-attractions-in-hanoi/

10 Delicious Foods to Try in Hanoi, Vietnam as Recommended by a Local - TripZilla.com

https://www.tripzilla.com/vietnamese-foods-try-hanoi/81939

10 Best City Center Hotels in Hanoi - Vietnam - Guide.com

http://www.vietnam-guide.com/hanoi/top10/top10-hanoi-hotels-city-center.htm

Do's and Don'ts - TravelHanoi.org

https://travelhanoi.org/do-and-donts/

Ultimate Travel Guide to Hanoi, Vietnam - DrewBinsky.com

https://drewbinsky.com/ultimate-travel-guide-hanoi-vietnam/

Timeline of Hanoi - Revolvy.com

https://www.revolvy.com/page/Timeline-of-Hanoi

A Look at Vietnamese Language, Culture, Customs and Etiquette - Commisceo - Global.com

https://www.commisceo-global.com/resources/country-guides/vietnam-guide

History Facts and Timeline - World - Guides.com

http://www.world-guides.com/asia/vietnam/hanoi/hanoi_history.htmlHanoi

The First - Timers Travel Guide to Hanoi, Vietnam - WillFlyforFood.net

https://www.willflyforfood.net/2017/08/28/the-first-timers-travel-guide-to-hanoi-vietnam/

Welcome to Hanoi - LonelyPlanet.com

https://www.lonelyplanet.com/vietnam/hanoi

www.ingramcontent.com/pod-product-compliance
Lightning Source LLC
Chambersburg PA
CBHW060516100426
42743CB00009B/1332